Mind's Power
Unleashed

Mind's Power Unleashed

A Guide to understanding why people do what they do

Sam Chauhan

iUniverse, Inc.
New York Lincoln Shanghai

Mind's Power Unleashed
A Guide to understanding why people do what they do

Copyright © 2007 by Sam Chauhan Companies

iUniverse books may be ordered through booksellers or by contacting:

iUniverse
2021 Pine Lake Road, Suite 100
Lincoln, NE 68512
www.iuniverse.com
1-800-Authors (1-800-288-4677)

Because of the dynamic nature of the Internet, any Web addresses or links contained in this book may have changed since publication and may no longer be valid.

The views expressed in this work are solely those of the author and do not necessarily reflect the views of the publisher, and the publisher hereby disclaims any responsibility for them.

ISBN: 978-0-595-44876-0 (pbk)
ISBN: 978-0-595-69057-2 (cloth)
ISBN: 978-0-595-89200-6 (ebk)

Printed in the United States of America

Special thanks to my wonderful parents, Desh and Kirin Chauhan. Your patience and encouragement were the fuel of my success. Also, thanks to my inspiring wife, Thelma and my children, Anali, Saria, and Sanjay for bringing me light into my life and reminding me to always nurture the spirit of a child within and putting up with my long hours.

Bill Criss, thank you for believing in me and giving me a special chance. A special thanks to Tom Hunt for giving me great advice, my special friends Ashwin Rajput, Fabian Garcia, Gregg Mullery, Robert Gomez, Josie Andrade, Arnulfo Ruiz, and my team. You guys stood by me when the going got tough.

Denise Serrano, thank you for stepping up each time I wanted you to step up and being there whenever I needed you. Ajay and Dorian, I greatly appreciate the hard work and long hours you've dedicated. A very special thanks to my grandfather for your wisdom and willingness to share your advice.

CONTENTS

INTRODUCTION

I want to share with you a secret. It might surprise you at first, so allow yourself to read it three or four times if you have to. That's normal. Ready? All you have ever dreamt of in life can be yours if you want it.

Actually, that's not so far-fetched after all, is it? I mean, you have dreamt up many things. And you have wanted them to a certain extent, haven't you? Maybe you just didn't want them to the extent of actually having them. Or perhaps you did get something that you wanted, but were you able to stand atop that mountain of accomplishment and earnestly bask in appreciation of the having? Chances are you might have skipped that step. You were already thinking about the "what's next," which you treated just the same.

But let's consider something you want badly enough and still haven't attained. It might be a particular kind of house. A mansion? A castle? It might be a car. A Porsche? A Ferrari? It might be a new career. A politician? An artist? It might be confidence. It might be a lean body. It might be a soul mate. It might be the feeling of extraordinariness.

"Yeah, yeah" you are telling yourself. "You're going to give it to me?" No, I'm not that boastful. I don't even know the exact thing that you want. And most likely I don't have it. All I can guess is that you want "something." That's an educated guess. We all want something. Perhaps this "something" that you want, you've wanted for a long time. That's a guess too. The thing is, you already have in your mind a picture of what this wonderful "something" is. It's just buried underneath all of this burdening thought of why you can't have it, thoughts about what's realistic and what's not, and thoughts about why you don't deserve to have it. I get that.

Let me give you something. A gift. *All the things you have ever dreamt of in life can be yours if you want it.* You might think that this statement is not mine to give. And you're right. But I understand what this means and I believe in it and I have manifested the things I have dreamt of in my life, so now I want to show you how you can understand and believe and manifest too. This gift can belong to everybody. I am only bringing it to light for you. I am only offering a genuine suggestion based on my own experience: Believe in this gift. And once you have it, this belief that you can have all the things you have ever dreamt of in life, give it to someone else. Don't worry, this doesn't mean you will lose anything. You take, you give, there never has to be any loss. There are enough dreams to go around for everyone.

Here is the way I live my life. I travel across the world as a highly sought speaker, teaching people how they can easily take control of their mind and achieve true success and fulfillment within their life and business. I am happy, I am productive, I am successful, and I am empowered. I can only imagine what my thirties will be like. I am not telling you this to show off. I am telling you this because these things are part of the dreams I have manifested in my life. I worked hard for them and believed in myself and now I am proud of what I have. Once you have made your dreams come true, you should be just as proud too.

My success is a reflection of myself and of what I learned to tell myself along with all the pivotal smart decisions I made along the way. And it was enough.

At eighteen years old I saw a commercial on TV about some inspirational tapes that promised to change my life "*now.*" I was fresh out of high school and enrolled in community college. In high school, I had performed poorly in most of my math classes so consequently picked up the habit of always looking for new ways to better myself and fine tune any skills in areas I lacked power. So I wrote down the number, grabbed my father's credit card and bought the tapes. I listened to them every day and made a bold decision. I would do something great. I would make a lot of money.

Although the subject matter was interesting, I started questioning my position in college. I was studying pre-law with hopes of eventually achieving great success and financial abundance. I liked the ideas about arguing boldly and making a difference, but I still wasn't accomplishing my dreams as quickly as I desired. Most of the jobs I had taken to pay for school and my car were in the retail circuit. I was always good a salesperson and had the ability of moving ahead then but it was a slow trek and the gains were not as satisfying as I wanted them to be. It was then that I decided to get a part-time job in a business where I might be able to move ahead to higher positions of power and access financial freedom.

I had one pair of nice shoes and two collared business shirts that I would rotate as I started going to interviews for telemarketing positions. I was repeatedly denied but persisted. One day as I was walking down the street from an interview at nineteen years old, I passed by a mortgage company and went in to inquire if there were any telemarketing positions available.

The receptionist responded with a "No." I looked around and noticed the placards on the wall and the business cards at the front desk, with individual pictures of loan officers all professionally dressed and appearing important, and I thought to myself: *Loan officers make a lot of money, right?*

I asked the receptionist if there was anyone I could speak with to learn about becoming a loan officer. She said that the only person in the office was the vice president but that I would have to make an appointment to speak with him since he was such a busy man. I asked her to please ring him and tell him all I needed was just a few moments of his time to simply ask some questions. She hesitated at first but then rang him anyway. He agreed to give me just a few moments.

When I met the vice president, I told him flat out that I had no experience and no knowledge of the loan business but that I was willing to learn everything. Fast. He told me, "If you had the guts to come in here and tell me this, then maybe you have enough for the job. But first, you have to do two things." The first thing consisted of establishing a list of fifty names. The names would have to be of people who were willing to process a home loan through my services. The second thing was that I would have to take classes on how the mortgage business worked. He gave me a date two months away: February 2nd. If I had these things completed by then, I would have a job.

That day I decided to quit pre-law and get to work. I went to everybody I knew, friends, family, old teachers, acquaintances, all to get the list of fifty names. I enrolled full time in mortgage business training classes and passed each one. By February 2nd, I had completed the two tasks and was sitting in my suit and tie in the lobby of the mortgage office awaiting my new job.

At first glance, the vice president didn't recognize me. He was baffled. He said he had given those two tasks to so many people, but that nobody had ever completed them in the two months. By the end of the day, I was officially part of the team and paving my new path to unfaltering success. It took three years of working in the business and studying Neurolinguistic Programming, a science of success you will learn about in this book, and at the ripe old age of twenty-two, I was the top producer of my company. Still, it was not always an easy journey as most journeys have their setbacks and rough patches. My parents always wanted me to go back to college regardless of how much determination I had. Learning to overcome someone else's beliefs in establishing your own is something you will read about in this book. When I first started working, I used to park my car blocks away because I was so embarrassed of my car. Now I have my own parking spot. This book will divulge the beliefs and the methods that have helped me realize my greatness so that you may realize yours.

I am not going to change your life.
This book is not going to change your life.
You are going to change your life.
How badly do you want it?

Sam Chauhan

PART ONE:
THINK DIFFERENT

CHAPTER ONE:
THIS MYTH CALLED
REALITY

"As far as the laws of mathematics refer to reality, they are not certain; and as far as they are certain, they do not refer to reality."

—*Albert Einstein*

What is reality? Is it the room you are in? Is it the ceiling in need of a new paint job? Is it the floor in need of another sweep? Is it the couch you're sitting on, the T.V. set you love, the books on the shelf or the garbage ready to be taken out? Is it your family, your children, your parents, your friends? Is it your job? Is reality the sleeping in or waking up or eating dinner or making coffee? Is it the trying to be on time, the paying for bills, the planning a vacation, the searching desperately for a perfect mate?

The truth is that "reality" is something we will never be certain about. It is devoid of an accurate definition. Reality, in actuality, does not exist. How we see the world is incredibly different for every single individual, because how we see the world is merely based on what is called perception. My perception and yours are two entirely different things. I can enter a room and call it large because I may have only experienced being in rooms smaller by comparison, so my perception will be based on that. You, on the other hand, may have been in several larger rooms in your past so the same room that may appear large to me will be small to you. That is perception. It is simple. Some people look at their lives and see accomplishment, success, health and wealth, love and respect, and the potential for more in the future. These are the people who live extraordinary lives. How do you see your life?

Our experience in this world is a funny thing. We are born without instruction manuals, babbling, totally vulnerable and receptive to our environments. As we grow, what we begin to believe as truth are fragmentary injections of words and pictures and stories from a variety of sources: our parents, our siblings, our schools, our friends, our television sets … the list goes on and on. Some of this information is good and empowering, but a lot of it is also limiting and disempowering.

We take all of this, making a concoction in our minds called "reality," and we start to live our lives in patterns and routines based solely on this so-called reality. Patterns and routines are the beginnings of living a mediocre life.

This reality can also be referred to as our internalized map of the world. Our perception is based on the five senses, sight, hearing, touch, taste, and smell. When we accept what we receive, which makes up our perception, our reality, our map, we are creating a distortion of the external world. A map is not an exact replica; it is only a version of the external thing, which is open for interpretation by all individuals. Still, a map offers possibility. Not only does it give you a version of what exists for you, it gives you possibility for what can exist. In order to have a map of endless possibility, a map that gives options of where you can be and what you can have, you must be willing to replace the limited, internal map that lives in your head. You must be willing to replace your stubbornness with insists on believing in it.

After all, does your reality even work for you? Do you feel you can accomplish anything you ever dreamed of? Do you feel confident and successful in every conversation, every business endeavor, in every step you take down the yellow brick road of your life? Do you feel energized and full of vitality? Do you feel joyous and enthusiastic? Do you feel empowered? Are you living a life of magnificence and sheer greatness? You can be. And you should be! There has never been any reason to think or feel otherwise. You only imagined there to be. Some imaginings are the beginnings of excellence, and others, like the ones that limit you, are not. This book is about attaining limitless excellence and personal power. This book is about manifesting joy and the dreamed of life.

So allow yourself to be selfish at the start. If you remove from your mind all negative associations with this word "self-ish," you can see the word blankly as representing one thing: to be concerned chiefly with one's own profit or pleasure. You can read from many relationship books, self-help manuals, or lifestyle magazines something that has almost become a cliché, that you are unable to love anyone else unless you love yourself first. So I'm asking you not to be selfish in the sense that you are going to walk all over people, use people, or to debilitate them, for these are all based on the learned negative connotations you already associate with the word. I am asking you to be selfish so that you ask yourself just what you truly desire and understand how important this idea is. Once you understand how important this is, that you have desire, that you have some thing or things that you have always wanted but have never acquired, you will be ready to decide that you must attain them. You will understand that there should never be any compromise in having what you want most. And you will be ready to resurrect from the depths of your reality, the depths of your mind, what has always been there: the answers on how to achieve your destiny.

In the crypts of London's iconic Westminister Abbey, the following words were written on the tomb of an Anglican bishop (1000 AD):

> When I was young and free and my imagination had no limits, I dreamed of changing the world. As I grew older and wiser, I discovered the world would not change, so I shortened my sights somewhat and decided to change only my country.
> But it, too seemed unmovable.
> As I grew into my twilight years, in one desperate attempt, I settled for changing only my family, those closest to me but alas, they would have none of it.
> And now as I lie on my deathbed, I suddenly realize: If only I had changed myself first, then by example I would have changed my family.
> From their inspiration and encouragement, I would then have been able to better my country, and who knows, I may have even changed the world. [1]
> Anonymous

Start with yourself.

---

[1]   Canfield and Hansen, *Chicken Soup for the Soul*, 72.

The psychological strategies of human beings mostly work in patterns and routines. A person's past is filled with good and bad experiences. A person's present is filled with the outcomes of his or her past, and they function on reacting instead of acting according to a limiting belief system. He or she will often repeat the same mistakes, answer questions the same way, end relationships the same way, or handle problems the same way. All this will ensure for the person's present and for his or her future, is the same of what they've already had in the past. By working in patterns and routines, a person will never fully grow because he or she will only keep getting more of what they already know, resulting in boredom and despair.

By recognizing patterns in your life and interrupting them, you can live from moment to moment, realizing how new each moment is, realizing you have choices and options on how to live your life and that you are in control. Being in control of your mind and your life is being powerful. New opportunities will start to open up for you once you admit: "I have driven this route home before and have always experienced delays, so therefore I will try a new route." New thoughts will begin to arise once you say to yourself: "I have reacted this way with my husband when he came home late in the past and it resulted in conflict, so therefore I will approach him with a new demeanor." A new life will be manifested for you once you acknowledge: "I have done this in the past and have felt disempowered, so therefore I am going to do something else." Stop living your life according to a limiting belief system! You are in control of that. You can stop at any time.

As previously stated, our perception is based on the fragmentary injections of something or someone else, and our belief systems are based on our distorted perceptions. Most beliefs were never chosen consciously. We chose them unconsciously. The bulk of our belief system was constructed when we were only children. Children are the most susceptible to other people's beliefs and ideas because their mind has not been fully bombarded with much of anything. It is new. A child's mind is a clean slate, vulnerable to everything that comes its way. The first few years of a child's life are crucial to his or her personal development. By age two, a child would have already reached 75 percent of brain growth[2]. This is the foundation of a belief system and this child's, this person's, reality. Some people based most of their belief system on what they learned from their parents, while others based most of theirs on what they learned at school. If your school was known for having a good athletics program and day in and day out, it was confirmed that athletics were important and meaningful, then most likely

---

2   Kassing, *Introduction to Recreation and Leisure*, 231.

you would continue believing that athletics were important and meaningful components to life. If a majority of students liked wearing Nikes, then your belief would be that wearing Nikes equals being cool. Later, this belief would morph into the thought that whatever the majority of people around you are wearing must be cool, so you will conform to be cool.

When you break down the word "belief," you will see the word "lie" right smack in the middle of it. I'd like to say that's because most beliefs are lies. Most people cannot understand that because the taught definition of "belief" is: something that you are certain about. And if you are certain about it, you believe this as truth. Just like reality, truth and beliefs are easily compromised, and most of what they are based on is the narrow-minded, dismantling version you've made of your world. This version insists that you be everything less than extraordinary.

The way you can start to understand this and achieve the dramatic replacement of your belief system is to accept the fact that there were certain beliefs in history that people thought to be true, then found out that they were not. Something so basic, but so utterly revolutionary is the idea that people once thought the world was flat. This was an accepted, worldly view. As accepted as we need oxygen to live, as accepted as every life results in death, something that did not seem possible of questioning. When many of us went to school, we were taught Pluto was a planet. Now we have found out this is untrue. If these things can be untrue, then why not other things in your life?

Chapter Two:
Rising Above
Mediocrity

"It's a sign of mediocrity when you demonstrate gratitude with moderation."

—*Roberto Benigni*

Do you like feeling comfortable? Is this a good word for you? Well, what if I told you that you are only comfortable because limiting belief systems based on patterns and routines (i.e. everything you already know) allow you to live this way? I am here to say something that may upset you at first. It might press your buttons, make you shake your head, and urge you to disagree with me because you like everything that comfort represents. You like familiarity, you like expectation, you like certain things you've gotten in the past and want more of them. What about everything else? What if you could feel

10 million times more satisfied with new things you've never even heard of before? A life of comfort will always result in a life of mediocrity because the human condition is to always want more. It is our inherent nature to reach, but it is sadly becoming our conditioned nature to be depressed and bored since all we ever reach for are the same things. We are conditioned to be fearful of failure because society tells us failure is the antithesis to happiness. Guess what? Society also taught you that word "failure." Failure, like reality, does not and has not ever existed. Pause and contemplate this. Everyone has made mistakes and experienced impediments. You can either go home, lie in bed, wail about it and call it "failure," or you can learn the lessons that have presented themselves, dust yourself off, and try again.

There is no such thing as failure, only feedback. This idea is a major component in the revolutionary science I will discuss in depth throughout this book: Neurolinguistic Programming or NLP. NLP is a set of techniques, axioms, and beliefs that are used as an approach to personal development. It was began in the early 1970's in California at the University of Santa Cruz by Richard Bandler, a student in information sciences and mathematics and Dr. John Grinder, a professor of linguistics. They studied people who had achieved excellence and developed skills on how to duplicate such excellence by modeling their language, physiology, and belief systems. Fundamentally, NLP states that we are all born with the same basic neurology. Our ability to do anything in life, whether it's riding a bicycle, boiling an egg, or reading this book depends on the way our nervous systems are being controlled. NLP is devoted to learning how to think more effectively and communicate more effectively with yourself and with others. You will become a master of these techniques when I relay them to you in the next part of this book. You will be able to replace your limited beliefs with the beliefs of those who you admire and achieve their successes and your own. However, you must be willing to forfeit your limiting beliefs and fears. Your reality, as you know it, is about to be altered.

Some years ago, I had an assignment to find people who had the limiting beliefs called "phobias." One night in Chicago I decided to go to McDonalds at 11:00 pm to find someone who wanted me to help them solve a problem of theirs. I saw a homeless man who appeared to be in his forties and asked him what had happened in his life that resulted in his current state. We both had had hardships in our lives, but he ended up homeless, and I ended up where I ended up, not homeless.

He told me that his wife had left him eleven years ago and this was devastating because he loved her deeply and she was everything to him. As soon as she left, he felt he had nothing else to live for. His wife even took his children away, destroying his whole concept of what a family represented, so he decided to do nothing. He accepted defeat and "failure" in his life. He stopped working and eventually started to live on the streets. He told me then that the streets had become his home. His phobia simply consisted of living a functional life since a functional life had caused him so much despair.

At this point in his story, I started working on reprogramming his brain, something you will learn about later in this book. When I was done, he told me: "I want to show you something." He left me and retreated to the restroom, then returned a few moments later, clean-shaven and smiling. He told me he had not shaven in years and appeared to be a new man. I made him do some affirmations, having him say to himself: "I am a powerful person." He told me then that he wanted to get a job and be able to see his children after eleven years. I gave him $100.00 so he could buy a decent outfit and apply for a job. That is how powerful a belief is, it could literally bring your life down or take it to a higher level in a matter of moments.

But it is up to you to allow a positive belief to live and grow functionally in your mind.

When you go back in history, you will see that people's beliefs are the causes of most wars. I need you to ask a question of yourself.

Do I have any beliefs that might not be true?

Just by asking yourself, you are going to open up new neuro pathways. That will be the start of being able to change some of these beliefs. What you believe to be true about yourself and about life in general determines the actions you will take in various circumstances, and also the actions you will not take. Your beliefs will predetermine your outcomes simply because of what you see as possible. Your beliefs will determine the possibilities you will consider for yourself in subsequent situations. If you can't imagine there being any communication in a relationship you're about to give up on, if you can't imagine yourself asking for a pay raise from an intimidating boss, if you can't imagine yourself making more money than so-and-so, or being thin and flawless like that girl on the magazine cover, or feeling enthusiastic about your career and joyous for no other reason besides being alive, start imagining. Imagination is your soul's way of remembering universal truth. And if you want to start believing in something that is certain, even if it is only certain to you alone, why not start with believing in yourself? Even if you're the only one who believes it, it is enough.

When things are not going well for you, a good place to start examining the situation is at the level of your beliefs. Ask yourself the following questions: What are my beliefs about this situation? And how can I adjust my beliefs to have a better outcome? If you believe that you deserve to be successful, most likely you will become successful. The problem here is that people think that just by believing they deserve to be successful, they will be successful. This is definitely a powerful step and one in the right direction, but it is only one step.

Once you believe you deserve success, you must act on it. You must turn your positive thought into a positive action, or else it will diminish, it will go unfed and unused and you might as well have never thought it if you are going to do nothing with it. Be outstanding. If you are outstanding, that means you stand out from the rest. The average human being is either dead or broke by age seventy. How sad is that? It is not an accident that 96 percent of wealth belongs to 1 percent of all people. The reason most people do not achieve all the things they want in life is because they have two beliefs stirring inside of them. One belief says you can do it, while the other one says you cannot. These are called conflicting beliefs. You get pulled in two directions and you end up doing nothing. What stops most people from achieving what they want is the belief that they can't have it.

I had a friend with many talents. He was a great speaker, he was funny, he had the ability to learn very quickly, and he was a good athlete. He could do all these things when there was no expectation put upon him. When he was left alone, he felt relaxed and could recite poems and deliver impromptu speeches. But the moment anyone complimented him, or he felt he was being watched, he could not perform even the simplest task. He stammered, forgot the lines, and instantly became a changed man. I could not understand this inconsistency. So I decided to explore his past and help him discover the reasons behind his ineffective behavior.

I discovered that when he was a child, his father always demanded perfection from him. When he came home with a mark lower than an A, he would be severely punished and called "stupid." To compensate for his poor self-image, my friend took on the role of the class clown. Throughout high school, he performed poorly in all subjects simply because he believed he was stupid. Whenever he knew he could do better, he stopped himself to remain consistent with the belief that he was a stupid person. He had let that belief linger in his mind for so long that it became a truth and in order for him to not think himself crazy and interfere with such truth, he had to live up to it, so he did. He was not aware of how powerful his negative beliefs about himself were.

When I confronted him with it, initially he was defensive and even angry. Only after some time, where we discussed it repeatedly, did he begin to realize that his negative self-image did not allow him to express his full potential. To help change his beliefs about himself, I conducted three NLP sessions with him, after which his life completely changed. My friend replaced his beliefs with new ones, that he was smart and able. All of a sudden, his business soared, his financial situation drastically improved, and he had found freedom in a new world of possibilities.

I wonder how many negative beliefs may hold you back from achieving what you are truly capable of. What do you believe about yourself? What do you believe you deserve to have? What are your beliefs about money? If I held onto my family's beliefs about financial rewards, I would have thirty years of waiting ahead of me. I wouldn't have taken the steps I took to not only become financially independent, but financially successful.

For a moment, let's examine various beliefs surrounding a child's poor performance in school, which you can easily translate into your level of success in everyday life. You can equate this situation with your career, your romantic relationship, or with your weight, whatever area you care mostly about.

When a child does poorly on an exam, the teacher, or whomever you feel is watching you, criticizing you, could say it is not his or her fault. Either it was the noise in the room or someone disturbed them. Here, the child would not feel responsible for the poor performance.

The teacher could also say, "You performed poorly on the exam." In this case, the teacher focused on a specific behavior, placing the responsibility on the student.

In another scenario, the teacher could say, "You are not very good at this material." Obviously, the implications of this belief would be different. If the student believes this message, he or she will most likely continue performing poorly on subsequent exams.

The most devastating statement would be, "You are just incapable of doing well." If the student adopted this belief at a core level, holding the highest respect for his or her teacher and accepting the teacher's statement as truth, this would have a devastating impact on this student's performance on all the tests. The whole being of this student would be deeply affected by this belief. Also a belief adopted at a core level is the most difficult one to change. People usually hold onto their beliefs and live their lives in a way that makes them consistent with their beliefs, as negative and disempowering as they can be.

The same situation can be evaluated in many different ways, resulting in different outcomes. There are as many beliefs as there are people. We should choose beliefs that allow us to express our full potential. We run our own brains and choose what we want to keep in there.

The challenge that most people who have limiting beliefs have is that they don't even realize they have limiting beliefs. If there is something that you have been trying for a long time but cannot seem to accomplish, you must change your approach. When the public tried to make a laughing stock out of Thomas Edison after his 9,999 attempts to invent the light bulb, he shot back with, "I have not failed. I've just found 9,999 ways that won't work." On the ten-thousandth try, he succeeded. There is no such thing as failure, only feedback. He got that. What keep people trying the same things over and over with hope that they will get different results are their beliefs. Albert Einstein called that insanity. Insanity may merely be a heap of limited beliefs. If you are trying to open a door for the last two years with the same key and it has not opened, you better change the key or the doorknob. Try something new!

Limiting beliefs are the beliefs that will stop you from going to the next level. These beliefs are poison to your goal of being successful. Some examples of limiting beliefs:

1.) I am not smart enough.

2.) I don't know the language.

3.) I only want to do things that I am comfortable with.

4.) Rejection is bad.

The truth is that most people who are successful are not the most intellectual people in the world. Instead of being highly knowledgeable in one or two topics, they instead have a fair amount of knowledge in a variety of them. This simply makes them more flexible and flexibility is key. Being flexible means that you are willing to do something different when you realize what you are doing is not working. Sounds simple enough right? As simply as it may sound, many people tend to just settle for something not working instead of trying a new way. They start to grow accustomed to things not working in their favor and thus lead unsatisfying lives. In order to succeed with everything I will teach you in this book and the fundamentals of NLP, you must be flexible. For instance, people who want to be successful will not let language barriers stop them. I did a lot of my business with the Hispanic community that was mostly Spanish speaking only. The one problem of being unable to speak their verbal language was conquered and replaced with the success of being able to communicate through unconscious rapport. You will learn this technique and how to master rapport in the next part of this book.

If you continue doing things that you are comfortable with, you will continue getting the results of your past. Are you even happy with the results of your past? If you continue doing this, your future will only be a duplication of your past and you might as well live the rest of your life with your eyes closed because you will have nothing to look forward to. The only time you grow is when you do things that make you feel uncomfortable. It's like when you are trying to build a muscle while lifting weights and your body trembles and throbs in discomfort. Most avoid trying new things to avoid discomfort and rejection. They take rejection very personally. All rejection means is that you are not yet ready for the situation. Rejection is not a summary of who you are as a person. It is not a statement on your appearance, the words you used, or the figure in your bank account. Perhaps you need a little more experience before you try again, whether you are applying for a job or asking someone out. Maybe you need to perform a bit more research, or maybe you need to apply somewhere else, or ask someone else out. Whether you will be ready in a month or two months or five minutes, the choice is up to you. Try again. That is all. Don't be attached to the outcome of a single rejection. People get hurt all the time when they are rejected. They allow a false belief of inadequacy to nurture their hurt feelings and they grow comfortable with not provoking rejection again. They submit to a life of mediocrity.

You must remember that there are two things that guide mostly every action in our lives: fear and faith. What fear and faith have in common is that they are both predictions of the future. The difference between fear and faith is that fear is a negative prediction of what is going to happen tomorrow and faith is a positive prediction. Most people do things out of fear. What is fear? F=false E=evidence A=appears R=real. Most people have a fear of rejection, fear of not being loved, or a fear of losing something dear to them. One thing can be absolutely certain about your fears—they will only drive you in the wrong direction. Most of our fears are deep rooted in our unconscious and our unconscious is often an underestimated thing, despite how important it is in our lives. Our unconscious mind not only plays a tremendous role in running our bodies, but it also has a dramatic impact on the results we get in our lives. Often times, you will consciously want life to be a certain way, or you will consciously want a particular thing. Something gets in the way that we cannot recognize and we do not attain what we consciously desired. What is that "something" that has gotten in the way? It is your unconscious mind deploring you. Your unconscious mind and your conscious mind need to be on the same wavelength in order for accomplishment to occur. The key to bringing your unconscious mind onto the same wavelength as your conscious mind is to understand how both minds work.

Conscious and Unconscious

Your conscious mind is basically the part of your mind that has awareness of the world around you and the processes occurring within you at any particular time. It controls your short-term memory, which is your memory of thoughts from minutes to hours ago. However, your conscious mind is only the tip of the iceberg since the unconscious mind holds the majority of the information that can either hinder us or propel us just as powerfully. Your conscious mind and your unconscious mind excel at different things and it's important to recognize what these things are so that you know which areas of the brain require work and reorganizing.

The conscious mind excels at logic, verbal language, mathematics, analysis, sequence processing and working linearly. The unconscious mind, on the other hand, excels at intuition, creativity, and storing memories, running your body and forming your emotions. If fear is deep rooted in your unconscious, it must be eliminated before you can believe in succeeding. If you want to take your life to the next level, you must do things out of faith, not fear.

I will share a story about two women who had similar challenges in life, but one of the women ended up with a life that was empowering and inspiring, while the other ended up depressed and feeling useless. The women were both involved with similar men who were appeasing and always told them what they wanted to hear, consequently leaving out a lot of truth. Ultimately, the two women got pregnant and begun to fantasize about living out the American Dream with each of these men, getting married, buying houses, living a life in unity and in happiness. The dream that was fantasized would not manifest for either of them. The men started lying and they were caught leading two lives, each man having gotten one other woman pregnant.

One of the women, Denise, saw hints throughout her relationship with her boyfriend but only when she saw him with the other woman did she believe it. She left him and refused him when he tried to win her back. Denise knew their relationship would never be healed since it was based wholly on dishonesty, but she also held onto hope that this man would still be a father to her child. Years passed and the man did not live up to her hopes and never decided to be an active part of his daughter's life. Regardless, Denise chose to put her energy and focus into her career and raising her daughter. With commitment to her focus, and faith that she would give her daughter a good life, she was able to thrive in her company, build herself a pleasing life, and ensure that neither she nor her daughter would ever have to go without any thing that they'd ever want.

The other woman, Jenny, was in denial that her American Dream would never be realized, despite her boyfriend being dishonest with her and leading a double life. She thought everything was her fault and that she deserved all of her misfortune. This was her belief system, rock solid since she was a girl. She stayed with him for many years but decided one strong day to finally leave. This was a positive action. However, she was inconsistent with her action. She descended into becoming a person who was very insecure and miserable with her life. She was fearful she would be alone forever and unable to raise her child successfully. So she started to search desperately for a new man, for any man who could fill her void. This didn't take much time and pretty soon she found herself with a man who seemed entirely different from the one who had caused her so much pain. She told herself she would not make the same mistakes that she made last time, the mistakes she believed had resulted in her boyfriend cheating on her. It wasn't long before Jenny was pregnant again, and eagerly gluing back together the pieces of her American Dream. A few months after he found out she was pregnant, this new man left her for another woman. Again, this woman descended into self-pity and began a pattern of having numerous affairs with several men, living in fear that her life would fall apart at any time, settling for a meager job she didn't like and barely supporting two children who had to watch her emotions and life constantly fluctuate.

The difference between Denise and Jenny is that they both held onto separate mindsets, regardless of the fact that they both had the same awful thing happen to them. Denise communicated the event to herself in a different way than Jenny did. Denise took a different road, one that led her to the city of success while Jenny remained in a rut of trying to find a man who wouldn't disappoint her, being unable to, and blaming herself in the process. While Denise continues to succeed and become more fulfilled, placing all her faith in herself, Jenny becomes less and less fulfilled as her negative patterns continue to bring her down since they are only based on fear. She lives a life that not only threatens to destroy her spirit, but also threatens to destroy the spirits of her children who learn from her. Jenny has become comfortable in her discomfort, the most dangerous aspect of comfort there is.

Another dangerous condition many people often grow comfortable with is that one depression. Many announce their depression casually to others, as if it's simply a feature of life they've arrived at, accepted, and continue to keep around no matter how detrimental it may be. One of the reasons they continue being depressed is because of this acceptance. They'll go to a doctor who will confirm this depression and assign them an expensive pill as a remedy. They'll go to a therapist who will let them lay on their couch and describe in detail every facet of their depression, digging deep into the emotional wounds that may have caused it, and instead of altering the moods of each memory, just letting them remain as they are, ever-vivid and hurtful. And then the person will go home still thinking about their depression, knowing the roots of it but not eliminating. They'll return to the therapist to talk about it more, getting nothing resolved, but building up a nice bill.

Depression is simply an emotional state that a person can jump into and out of. It doesn't mean that a person who has it is incapable of happiness. Everybody is capable of happiness. Everyone is capable of depression. It's merely a matter of preference. People who are depressed are constantly carrying around bold images in their mind of why they are depressed, this macroscopic view of grief. They hold it so taut in their minds, they are so transfixed by it that it becomes their way of life and they become comfortable. It's easy to become comfortable with a way of life we have known for a little or a long while, especially if we have evidence and doctor's opinions that confirm these negative thoughts. Do yourself a favor and hold a positive thought in your mind. Gather evidence to confirm that you have choices on which mental preference you can have. Let the rest of the information I offer be some of your evidence.

Chapter Three:
The Power of Action

"The ancestor of every action is a thought."

—*Ralph Waldo Emerson*

Try something new. Tomorrow when you wake up in the morning, make a decision every step along the way. If you usually brush your teeth before washing your face, wash your face first. Then if you really want to tickle your brain, brush your teeth with your left hand if you usually brush with your right. If you're left-handed, do the opposite. Just by interrupting a routine as simple as brushing your teeth, you are stimulating a powerful facet of your mind—the facet of choice. You can react to your morning and your life or you act on it. You have a choice to live in every moment, so live. You have a choice to be successful, so be successful.

Most people think that success is something you have to chase. This is not true. What happens when you chase a butterfly? It keeps fluttering from you, flower to flower. This is the same case with success. You are not meant to chase success, you are meant to attract it. Consider the Law of Attraction: Like attracts like. Just like people who feel depressed and have the papers and medications and dreary looks to prove it, you can have accomplishment and success and love and happiness in your life if you have these things constantly stirring in your mind. Men and women who "get things" are constantly sending out strong waves of positive thought vibrations, which in effect attract the physical reality of their thoughts. They manifest.

Values and beliefs are the internal systems we cling to which affect every decision that we make. They allow us to discern what is "good or bad" or "right or wrong" based on what we have been taught by other people, by institutions, books, etc. etc. It is because of your values specifically that you either do or do not. And then after you do or do not, you use your values again to re-evaluate your situation and come to another conclusion about whether you should have or shouldn't have. For example if you strongly value honesty, you may find a forgotten purse in a subway car but turn it into the police and then praise yourself for doing so.

Your values are generally formed over the first part of your life so that well into adulthood you will have a solid foundation of what you consider to be of value to you. From the time of your birth to around seven years old, you will learn largely unconsciously from your parents. From age eight until thirteen, you will learn by consciously or unconsciously copying friends. Around ten years old, some of your core values are formed. Between the ages of fourteen and twenty-one, you will learn about values that affect your relationships with other people.

Sometimes we will experience a conflict of values when you consciously want to move toward an outcome, but your unconscious mind has other ideas about moving you away from your outcome and toward something else. This is based on the conscious and unconscious battle. There can also be a conflict when we simultaneously want two things at once. You may be at a friend's house and notice an unwrapped gift you had spent a lot of money on some months back. It is thrown in the corner and obviously unappreciated. One value will tell you that your gifts deserve more appreciation so you will want to take it back. Another value will tell you that once you give a gift, you cannot take it back. You will be in a state of suspension, trying to decide which value is true and more meaningful.

Although our values are mainly established when we are young, there is still possibility for changing them if you find that they hold you from getting things that you want. When you think of your values, you create an image just as you do with beliefs. If you are able to change the image that each of these values create, you will be able to change the hierarchy of your values. For instance, you might place your values in a hierarchy that looks like this:

1.) Accomplishment

2.) Health

3.) Family

4.) Fun

5.) Respect

If this is so, you might feel very accomplished in your life and proud of yourself, but you lack respect from other people, so it has a tendency to bring you down. This is when you must decide to swap something like fun for respect so that you can give the acquiring of respect just as much attention as you had given "fun." You will learn in the next part of this book about how to change images in our minds so that we can change our thinking patterns and consequently our results in life. The image of "fun" will become less vivid, less bold and bright and attractive an option than the image of "respect," which will step up in the hierarchy as something visually more pleasing and hence more important.

Let's talk more about beliefs. I want you to understand just how fundamental beliefs are and how they affect every aspect of your life. Beliefs are convictions that certain things are true or real. They are also generalizations about the state of the world. Beliefs are the presuppositions that create or deny personal power for us. Your beliefs are on/off switches for your ability to take actions. If you don't believe you can do something, you probably won't have the opportunity to find out. Perhaps the most important belief is your belief about beliefs. If you believe that you can choose and change your beliefs, you have personal power and are able to make massive changes in your reality. Let's examine beliefs held by all the most successful people in the world. These beliefs have helped countless people achieve excellence in their respective professions. I chose to adopt them and in the next part of this book, you will learn to master the specific methods of duplicating not only their belief systems, but also the successes their beliefs triggered in their lives.

Belief # 1: There are no failures, only lessons.

Successful people do not believe in failure. Failure is not part of their vocabulary. When things do not go the way they expect, they evaluate the situation, examine what worked and what didn't, learn from the experience, redesign the strategy, and move on, empowered by the lesson. Successful people always look for new ways to get better results until they find the very best one, as was the case for Thomas Edison and his light bulb.

Results are just reflections of strategies. We always get some sort of result. The quality of our results directly depends upon the quality of our strategies. The quality of a strategy has nothing to do with who we are. A lot of people make a critical mistake. They equate an undesirable result with personal inadequacy. They become a "failure" in their minds. But remember "failure" is only a learned word and a learned representation and is not true or real. Imagine a child learning to walk. If the child accepted this false concept of failure, he or she would never attempt to take another step. The child would never learn to walk, discouraged by the fall, and would feel incapable of learning everything else along the way. So to think as a child, to approach what seems to be a complex task with simple childlike hope and possibility, one might discover much more capability in himself than was ever considered.

This lesson applies to every aspect in life. When things go well, learn from the experience and repeat the strategy that led you to success. When things do not go well, re-evaluate your strategy and change the part that did not work. It's that simple. I do this all the time. When I operate my life, whether it be at business or at home, I closely examine the language I use when talking to myself. I change this language to success syntax. I reject ineffective words that are only labels anyway. I reject "failure," "inability," "difficulty," "problems," "depression," "sadness," and the notion that someone or something did something unjust to me. That is a huge thing, being able to take responsibility for your life. Playing the blame game can be easy and it will attract things like sympathy and wrinkled eyebrows but when it comes down to it, it still won't get you what you want. I am in charge, I am a learning machine, I am capable and powerful, I am in control and able to change my outcomes, I can change my feelings, I can change my beliefs, I can redesign my life. In other words, I can! Can you?

Belief # 2: Everything happens for a reason and the reason is to help us find the right path.

Successful people always look for possibilities in every situation. They look at life as a series of lessons and opportunities to learn something new, even when they experience the most adverse situations. When I think of successful people, I think of Abraham Lincoln. Most people don't know his story:

He failed in business in 1831.

He was defeated for state legislator in 1832.

He tried another business in 1833. It did not succeed.

His beloved fiancée died in 1835.

He had a nervous breakdown in 1836.

In 1843, he ran for Congress and was defeated.

He tried again in 1848 and was defeated again.

He tried running for the Senate in 1855. He lost.

The next year he ran for Vice President and lost.

In 1859 he ran for the Senate again and was defeated.

In 1860 he was elected President of the United States and has served as an iconic American hero ever since.

Imagine what his belief structure was. He always went forward. That is an exceedingly powerful key in life—to keep going forward.

Lance Armstrong is another example of a possibility thinker. As a cycling world champion, he was diagnosed with terminal testicular cancer and the public thought he would give up and that it would be perfectly understandable. The cancer then spread to his lungs and his brain. Given three months to live, Armstrong summoned his personal power and entered into treatment to beat the disease. When he recovered, he discovered his body was leaner, giving him an edge in mountain races. A year after his recovery, he won his first Tour de France, followed by six subsequent wins. He went down in history as the greatest cyclist who has ever lived. In the process, he gave hope to other cancer patients. Today, he raises millions of dollars for cancer research, turning his near-death experience into an opportunity for hope.

Armstrong credits his recovery from cancer and his Tour de France wins to having an unwavering belief in his outcomes. Before recovery, he already knew he would recover. He also knew he would become the Tour de France Champion. His conviction in his outcomes was so strong that in his mind the outcomes were factual, before they had even been manifested the world. This is the strength of belief.

Take a moment to examine your beliefs. Take a closer look at a particularly challenging situation in your life. Yes—that one! You know which one it is. Is there anything positive in the situation? If the situation happened in the past, ask yourself if there was a good outcome from the experience. All situations contain the seeds of opportunity. I once had a business partner who did not fulfill his end of a bargain. A significant amount of money was lost. At the time, I was very angry and disappointed, not only in my business partner but in myself for putting faith in him. In retrospect, I am satisfied. I learned something about reading people. I know I will never make the same mistake again which is a great lesson when large amounts of money and time are involved. In the long term, I am better because of the experience. Once you have decided to adopt the belief that every situation contains seeds of success, you will find out how easy it is for you to make positive changes in your life and in your business.

Belief # 3: I attract everything that occurs in my life.

This belief may be the hardest to accept. You may ask yourself, "How did I attract that accident, or that crash in the stock exchange, or any other misfortune I had no control over?" But the law of attraction always works. Like attracts like. Successful people are not immune to misfortune. They simply place themselves in the center of the situation, taking a vital position that allows them to be in charge of changing an outcome, no matter what the situation is. They refuse to accept a notion of helplessness. They refuse to passively accept the position that something or someone did something unjust or debilitating to them. Even in the most adverse circumstances, they know they can control something and have a choice to take action to turn the situation into an opportunity for success.

I have read various stories about survivors of war and destruction. Most survivors credit their survival to be being able to maintain a positive outlook. According to Edna J. Hunter, "It is probably the person who early in life developed a positive outlook, who can see alternatives in outcome in almost any situation, no matter how bleak, and who continues on in spite of the odds against him, who makes it through."[3] Some have said that amidst the horrors, they felt a sense of overwhelming peace and discovered true nobility in the human spirit. They spoke of acts of heroism on the part of their friends, acts of mercy on the part of strangers, and opportunities to test

3   Meichenbaum, *Human Adaptation to Extreme Stress: From the Holocaust to Vietnam*, 168.

their own strength under these most difficult circumstances. Following their liberation, many victims of war and destruction pursued successful careers. Successful people remain in full control. They take the position that they are the creators of their world and that they can change their reality. They know they are in charge of their brains and their beliefs and their worlds. This does not mean that they are immune from pain. It means they take charge when challenges occur. It means they have the strength to move on.

Sylvester Stallone is a prime example of this concept. He knew what it meant to be strong and move on. Having known throughout his whole life that he wanted to inspire others, he made a point of settling for nothing less than that. He wanted to be a film star and was reportedly rejected in over 1,500 auditions before landing a role. Some of the same agencies or companies dismissed him eight or ten times each. That is persistence. He finally got a role of being a thug but didn't like it. It wasn't inspiring enough. He did three films playing the same kind of character, hoping his exposure would land him more roles and in different genres. Still he kept getting rejected from the roles he truly wanted. So he changed his approach and stopped taking roles he didn't like and only going to auditions for roles he really wanted. Money stopped rolling in, the heat was turned off in his apartment, his wife constantly nagged him to get a job, but he knew if he accepted another thug role, even if he had money, he wouldn't have the satisfaction of acquiring his dream. He purposely burned all his bridges so he would have no other choice but to go after his dream. He knew if he had hunger, he would have drive. He would have persistence to seek nothing other but the fullest extent of what he wanted most.

He found himself in numerous arguments with his wife about money and in a state of distress when he was home in his cold and humble apartment. This inspired him to make a significant decision one day. He went to the public library where it was warm and started to read a book by Edgar Allen Poe. He took from this book the crucial point that had always lingered inside of him, that his purpose in life was to touch other people and to inspire them at any cost. It was the one thing he truly wanted. So he told himself that he would become a writer. He was totally broke, but started working on a script. When it was completed, he sold "Paradise Alleys" for a modest hundred bucks. He was most invigorated with the accomplishment in itself, rather than the monetary value of it.

Of course, a hundred dollars and the satisfaction of having only accomplished one dream only lasts so long. At one point,

Stallone became so broke that he had to sell his wife's jewelry. Then she eventually left him. The one thing that he felt most unconditionally loved by since his wife was gone was his dog. Still his financial situation was so bad, he resorted to having to sell it. He found himself at a nearby store trying to sell his dog to a complete stranger for $50.00 but he could not. One guy finally negotiated with him to buy his dog, Stallone's best friend, for $25.00. He accepted the measly payment, walked away and cried. Two weeks later, he was watching a fight between Muhammad Ali and this white guy who's getting beat up but who keeps coming back, retaliating. This one fight, this one experience, this one moment sparked an idea in Stallone's mind. He finished the screenplay for "Rocky" in 20 hours.

After trying to sell the script to several companies, he finally found someone willing to buy it for a satisfactory price. They offered him $125,000 for the script, but before accepting he told the producers that he needed to play the leading role and that would seal the deal. They refused at first, telling him he was a writer, not an actor. Sylvester told them, on the contrary, that he was Rocky and he was born to play the part. They entered their own match at that point, the producers vs. Stallone, with demands instead of fists. The producers told Stallone that they didn't just want an "anybody" for the role, and that they had already picked out Ryan O'Neil as Rocky. They gave him the choice to take the $125,000 for the script and settle or take nothing. Stallone took nothing. He refused to settle. He made a powerful choice. Imagine you having no money and leaving $125,000 on the table.

A few weeks later, Stallone received a call and was offered $250,000 but he would still not be able to star in his own film. He turned that down too. The final offer was $325,000, but alas he continued to insist that the producers allow him to play the role of Rocky. They finally came to a compromise with him. They offered him the leading role and the amount of $35,000 for his script. They assured him that the movie would most likely flop, but at least they wouldn't lose much and would be taking a chance. The first thing Stallone did with the money was track down the man to whom he'd sold his dog. He found him, offered him $100.00 and begged to have his dog back. The man refused to sell it. Then he offered $500.00. Still, the man refused. Even $1,000.00 got the same response and a guarantee that the dog would never be for sale. Of course, this guarantee was overturned when Stallone offered the man $15,000.00 to have his dog back. The dog you see in the cult classic Rocky I is his real dog.

What would you have done in this position?

Belief # 4: Work is fun!

Successful people love what they do. Period. Though they spend a lot of time on their endeavors, they do not view work as a chore. They have fun doing what they do so that "work" in their minds represents something entirely different from what the majority of people see and understand. Ask any great performer or billionaire businessman what stands as the one critical component of their success. Every single time, uncompromised, they will tell you that they have fun doing what they do. They are happy to wake up every morning and have their work ahead of them. Some of them don't want to take vacations because they enjoy their work so much. Successful people feel inspired by their work and they are constantly upgrading themselves, learning new things about their business, and trying new ways to do it better. They do not differentiate between their lives and their work. They view their work as their lives and this is not a negative thing, this is not a sad thing, as long as their work equals their passion, as long as they love doing what they do. If someone is referred to as a "workaholic," this is seen as a negative concept. "Bob is a workaholic, he never has time for himself." Is Bob also happy? If Bob is a workaholic, and his work is his passion, if his work makes him happy because he is doing what he loves and accomplishing his dreams, then call him a "passion-holic." Our concept of Bob is not so sad after all. Being a workaholic is only an undesirable thing if you are stuck in a job you hate. You are not following your dreams.

Ask Donald Trump if he takes vacations or when he is planning to retire. He would tell you that he never takes holidays because he loves his business, and he never plans to retire because his work is play for him. I love my business. I cannot wait to get up in the morning and start my day. Every day is a new, exhilarating challenge. I am always learning, always asking questions, and always networking with people who have common interests. This is the only way to truly succeed. When you equate your work with pleasure, you are guaranteed to succeed beyond your wildest dreams, because you are finally in sync with them.

Belief # 5: Commitment is the key to success.

The most essential belief held by all successful people is that there is no success without commitment. Commitment comes from an unfaltering belief in the desired outcome. When I talk with some of the most successful people on this planet, they tell me that in their minds, the outcome they envision is already a fact, long before it is manifested in the physical world. They fill in he blanks between Now and the goal that already exists in their mind. In other words, you must feel right now have you would feel if you had already accomplished your goal. You create your reality this way, long before it shows up.

Successful people share the "no matter what" attitude. No matter how hard it may be, no matter how long it may take, no matter what other people will say or think, no matter what challenges may occur, successful people persevere. Nothing comes between them and their dreams. They are totally committed to their results.

Empowering beliefs are beliefs that will empower you to excel in the game and take you to your next levels. Some of your empowering beliefs should look like the ones stated above or like these affirmations:

1.) I am smart!

2.) I could accomplish anything I desire!

3.) I am strong!

4.) I will not fail!

5.) I am an amazing person!

People always stop and ask me, "How do you replace your limiting beliefs with empowering beliefs?" I make this happen in my seminars where I have everybody write down their limiting beliefs on a wood board made out of pine. I teach them how to break through the board and the limiting beliefs that they have. It doesn't matter if they use their hands or a hammer, their mind will remember that it was responsible from breaking it and breaking down its limiting belief system. On the following lines, write down your own limiting beliefs:

1.)_____

2.)_____

3.)_____

4.)_____

5.)_____

Now write down the empowering beliefs you would like to have.

1.)_____

2.)_____

3.)_____

4.)_____

5.)_____

The way you will instill empowering beliefs is by reading them out loud every morning to yourself. This will be an interruption of your mental reactions. You can equate it with being told that the exit ramp you usually use to get home is now closed after you have been using this exit, routinely, for the past four years. You'll have to exit a different way and find a new route home. After ten to fifteen times, this new route will be accepted, your neurons will create a new pathway, and your taking it will become automatic. Life will change for you. You will have made a choice. Make your empowering beliefs your permanent ones.

Where would your life be if you got rid of your limiting beliefs and installed empowering beliefs?

_____

_____

_____

_____

_____

What would be things you would have in your life if you knew failure was not possible?

_____

_____

_____

_____

_____

_____

_____

Study the list above. It constructs a skeleton for what you believe to be an extraordinary life. Everything you would have if you didn't believe in failure. In one moment, this one here, be informed that failure no longer exists. Seize.

Chapter Four:
The Big Q

"It is better to know some of the questions than all of the answers."

—James Thurber

Who? What? When? Where? Why? How? Who writes their report better? What do they do different from me? When will I change my approach so that I may succeed? Where will I learn this? Why is this important? How will I complete this task? Successful people always understand the power of questions. If you ask the right question, you get around any situation. If you want to start a business, but do not have enough start up money, how will you find a way? Sitting on the couch and turning on the television? Having a drink? Discussing with a friend the details of this impossible task? Or will you make a plan? Will you decide to get what you want at all costs?

Consider for a moment the story of an African-American woman born to teenaged, unwed parents, and raised by her grandmother on a Mississippi farm for the first six years of her life. For the exceeding years, from age six to thirteen, this girl was sent to live with her mother in Milwaukee during which time she was raped by her cousin at age nine and continuously molested by a male friend of her mother's and by her uncle. Ashamed, the girl never told anyone about the abuse, but chose instead to rebel. She repeatedly ran away and found trouble.

At this point, the girl's mother decided to send her to a detention center but she was denied because there was no vacancy. Consequently, she was sent to live with her father in Nashville, which was a much stricter environment. Before truly adhering to her father's rules, she became pregnant and gave birth to a stillborn baby at the mere age of fourteen. The devastation of this experience combined with her father's strict household rules started to turn this girl's life around. Her father made her read a book a week and write a book report at the end of each one. At the age of nineteen, this girl landed her first job as a reporter for a local radio station in Nashville. Shortly after, she began her studies in radio and television broadcasting at the University of Tennessee. In 1976, this young woman moved to

Baltimore to host a television show called "People are Talking." It was an immense hit and she remained on-air for eight years. Then she was approached to do her own morning talk show in Chicago. She accepted and it was an even bigger success. She was offered a role in a Steven Spielberg film, nominated for an Oscar, and in 1986 her show was re-named "The Oprah Winfrey Show." The rest is history. Oprah came from being a poor, black farm girl in Mississippi to being a national celebrity. On top of her title "talk-show host," Oprah has also earned the prestigious titles of reporter, actress, writer, producer, and activist. She is an icon for success. And you can be assured that she asks herself from time to time the following question, "What can I do better?" And then she does it.

When the cards of life are dealt against you, it does not mean you cannot win. If you ask yourself the right question, there is no obstacle that you cannot get around. There are two types of questions you can ask yourself, the disempowering and the empowering.

Disempowering questions:

1.) Why am I an idiot?

2.) Why doesn't anybody like me?

3.) Why am I not beautiful?

4.) Why do I have no money?

The problem with these questions is that your brain will find an answer. If you ask yourself, "Why am I an idiot?" your brain will search for an answer and find one that is untrue and disempowering. You will answer yourself with, "You are an idiot because you make bad decisions." How does that answer help you make better decisions in the future? It doesn't. That is why a question like this is called a disempowering question. When you attempt to make a decision in the future, your brain will have told you that you only make bad ones, so automatically you will perceive any decision you make to be bad since that's what you believe you are only capable of making. If you ask yourself, "Why do I have no money?" your brain will answer with, "You have no money because you are an idiot." Now what do you do? You keep having no money, you keep seeing your decisions are bad, and you keep living a life of misery that you will never be happy with. It is essential that you ask yourself empowering questions.

Empowering Questions:

1.) How can I attract more quality people in my life?

2.) What can I do to make more money?

3.) How can I learn more?

4.) What are some of the amazing things I have done?

If you can master asking yourself better questions, then you will be able to get the results you want in your life. This all starts with you. Are you up for the challenge? If you have children, don't ask yourself, "Why is my child a bad speller?" Instead, ask yourself, "How can I help my child become a better speller?"

What are some of your disempowering questions? Write down 10 that you repeatedly ask yourself.

_____

_____

_____

_____

_____

_____

_____

_____

_____

What are some of your empowering questions? Write down 10 that you should repeatedly ask yourself.

_____

_____

_____

_____

_____

_____

_____

_____

_____

_____

The way you can make sure that you are creating a functional practice on asking yourself empowering questions is by consistently looking at what you have written down and by using the tool of repetition to reinforce them. Ask powerful questions to get powerful results.

Once you've asked yourself what you want and successfully answered it, formulate a new question: "What will that do for me?" Repeat the question to yourself so that you locate the core value of this decision and specify exactly what you are considering. If you don't do this, you might just jump on the first few things you "want" which may just be surface options atop a vast possibility of your true goal in mind. By being as specific as possible, you will be able to make more effective plans. For example, I had a good friend James who was a successful loan officer but evaluating his position in his career. In setting his goals, he had quickly decided that he simply wasn't making enough money or feeling empowered enough, so he would find a position in a new company. I suggested that he ask himself repeatedly the question: "What will that do for me?" He answered himself with, "More money and power." Then in continuing to question himself, he added to his answer, "It will also steal a lot of my time and energy since I will have to prove my ability at a new job." In repeating the question again and again, he was able to re-evaluate the situation and since all he wanted was more money and more power, he simply went to his superior at the job he already had and asked for a promotion and raise. With much evidence to support his abilities and since they were able to confirm this having tracked his progress within the company, he got exactly what he wanted through a completely different, but more effective route.

Be sure to question everything. Question yourself. Question your environment. Question books. Question philosophy.

Know that everything is open for interpretation. What about the questions we ask other people? You will learn more about this when we master rapport in the next part of this book but know that just as often as we question ourselves, we question other people. An important point to be made, whether you are asking yourself or someone else a question, is that it should always be clear and concise. How often to you ask questions that are only based on your map of the world and according to what you want? If you hear yourself asking questions that sound like commands with words such as "you must, you should, you can't," then you might be directing all of the action and imposing your ideas on somebody else. Be careful! Generally, if you ever have doubts about whether your question is appropriate to helping a person or situation move on to a someplace productive, stop and ask yourself: "Will my question add value to this conversation? Will this question bring us closer together or further apart?" Then you are predetermining the result or outcome of having asked the question. You are becoming a master of questioning and won't ever want to stop. Don't stop. Be like a student, never too knowledgeable to learn something new.

CHAPTER FIVE:
TALKING TO YOURSELF

"The words that enlighten the soul are more precious than jewels."

—Hazrat Inayat Khan

Today, the average adult vocabulary is estimated to be around 40,000 to 50,000 words. Whether we write some words more than we speak them, whether our ear canals receive some words more than our mouths generate them, what matters most are what these words, regardless of whether they're written, heard, or said, represent in our minds. You might have some words that are on constant repeat in your head, words that make up your beliefs. You might use your mouth to say words day in and day out that keep you in a state of suspension, in a negative reality. Our vocabulary is a part of our language, and our language is our way of expressing to the world and ourselves who we are, what we believe, what we want, and where we are going. If you are constantly using negative, disempowering words, then the visual representations associated with these words will imprint in your mind images of disempowerment. You will have all this clutter in your mind and consequently in your life of despair and hopelessness and mediocrity and boredom and anger and a variety of other limiting components. It's time to clean up.

The words you use daily affect how you feel and act so pay close attention to them. We may think that words only describe meanings, but they actually create your reality. Hearing a simple word like "lemon" might trigger your saliva glands, thus affecting your physiology. Reading the mere name of a lost loved one you haven't thought of in a while might trigger your tear ducts, provoke memories, affecting how you feel and what you say and do thereafter.

There are some words called generalizations that eliminate alternative choices and limit you from many things. These words are: all, everything, and never. You might use sentences like these:

1.) ALL my friends are more successful than I am.

2.) I tried EVERYTHING and I still cannot lose my excess weight.

3.) I will NEVER succeed.

These words allow you to give up. They express generalizations you've made out of situations and they eliminate all
possibilities for change or growth. Another set of words that
limit you are words of possibility. Words of possibility require
a particular action that may or may not be taken. They might
appear to be positive words, but these words can easily remain
just as thoughts, as plans, as ideas, and it is entirely up to you
whether or not you will catapult these words into concrete
action. Words of possibility include: should, can, and going to.
Perhaps you use sentences like these:

1.) I SHOULD ask Tina how she did so well on her exam.

2.) I CAN make more money.

3.) I'm GOING TO go to start going to the gym.

Although they are statements that point you in the right
direction and present specific tasks that may be helpful and
result in positive outcomes, the only way you will see these
positive outcomes are if you combine each of these statements
with action. All you are saying with these statements is that
you will get things done at your earliest convenience. When
we live our lives as erratically as we do, an earliest convenience

is almost the hardest thing to locate. Waiting for your earliest convenience is simply not being consistent. Replace the question of whether or not something is possible, with the question of: Are you willing to find out? Use words of necessity.

Words of necessity cut off all options and leave you no other choice but to act and complete the desired task. Although having choices and options are fundamentally good, choosing to do nothing about your desires and dreams can be hauntingly negative. When it is decided that you want something, cut out your options of dismantling yourself and choosing to do nothing, and give yourself the one choice to get what you want. Words of necessity are: must, have to, and need. It would be beneficial to use sentences like these:

1.) I MUST ask Tina how she did so well on her exam.

2.) I HAVE TO make more money.

3.) I NEED TO go to the gym today.

And then you must follow through. The next steps should be immediate. You realize that you must ask Tina how she did so well on her exam, so the obvious action would be to go ask. And once you ask, there will be a new opportunity to act, perhaps take notes from her to model her success. After you realize that you have to make more money, take the necessary steps to ensure that you will. If you know you need to go to the gym, if you think it and say it, then get up, put on your gym clothes, grab a bottle of water, and get moving. Let positive words and thoughts become your catalysts for a change in thought and a change in life altogether.

This does not mean that you cannot ever express dissatisfaction with something. Expressing dissatisfaction is not negative, but doing nothing with your dissatisfaction is. Sometimes if you use words like "angry" and "afraid" over and over again, you will find that you can do nothing with them, that the words paralyze you and give you no choice but to remain in a rut, saturated in all the negative images you associate with these words. If you simply change the words, you will find that their power is lessened and you will feel less intimidated and free to seek a satisfying, and more desirable state. For instance, if you often use the word "angry," replace it with "disenchanted." You can say something like, "I am disenchanted that I got a parking ticket," instead of, "I am angry that I got a parking ticket." This might sound ridiculous to you, like disenchanted is too bulky and unusual a word. It only seems this way to you because you do not use it as frequently as you do "angry." Ignore the idea that one seems to hold more intensity than the other, for "angry" and "disenchanted" more or less mean the same thing: dissatisfaction. No doubt about it, getting a parking ticket is a dissatisfying situation, and once it is left blaring on your vehicle's windshield, it seems there isn't much you can do but complain and kick yourself and pay the fine and be done with it. If you were in the wrong and must pay a fine, then what's the use of complaining and kicking yourself and allowing the negativity of the situation churn inside of you, being powerful enough to affect the rest of your day? Once you use the word "angry," whether you shout it aloud or flash it over and over in your head, "Oh I am so angry!" the visual images of what that word "angry" represents to you come piling in and filling you up with all the negativity of every experience in which you've ever felt "angry." The visual representation of such an overused, negative word is so powerful that simply by using it, you are tapping into a mountain of distress. The statement, "I am disenchanted I got a parking ticket," allows you to express your dissatisfaction, learn a valuable lesson such as "I will never park here at this hour again," and move on.

The following list is a power vocabulary that will assist you in using more useful and less incapacitating words so that your experiences with dissatisfaction will become opportunities for growth and change rather than moments of paralysis. Changing the words on the left for the words on the right will change the feelings these words provoke and help you develop your power vocabulary:

POWER VOCABULARY I

1.) Angry	Disenchanted
2.) Afraid	Uncomfortable
3.) Anxious	A little concerned
4.) Confused	Curious
5.) Depressed	Not on top of it
6.) Disappointed	Under whelmed
7.) Disgusted	Surprised
8.) Embarrassed	Stimulated
9.) Exhausted	Recharging
10.) Failure	Stumble
11.) Fearful	Curious
12.) Hurt	Bothered
13.) Humiliated	Uncomfortable
14.) Nervous	Energized
15.) Overwhelmed	Busy

However, a power vocabulary doesn't have to be used to express dissatisfaction only. By using synonyms for overused positive words, you can truly feel what you are saying each time you feel something good and say so. You can tap into new levels of fulfillment every time. If you say, "I feel happy" over and over and over again, happiness will quickly become boredom because the word will lose its impact on you. Below is a power vocabulary for positive words so that your statements will be fresh and fulfilling every single time.

POWER VOCABULARY II

1.) Happy   Ecstatic

2.) Attractive   Gorgeous

3.) Confident   Unstoppable

4.) Curious   Fascinated

5.) Enthusiastic   Excited

6.) Excited   Elated

7.) Fantastic   Fabulous

8.) Good   Dynamite

9.) Great   Phenomenal

10.) Alert   Energized

11.) Intense   Laser-like

12.) Interesting   Captivating

13.) Loved   Adored

14.) Motivated   Juiced

15.) Quick   Explosive

This is when a pocket thesaurus might come in handy for you. Carry one around for moments of great emotion or for whenever you are moved enough. It doesn't matter if it is an upsetting situation or an uplifting one. Just as you start to automatically utter some overused word to express yourself, pull out your thesaurus or this Power Vocabulary and utter something new. I guarantee you will feel something entirely different. You will feel the essence of possibility.

How about the way we string our words and statements together to communicate what happens to us? Your Power Vocabulary will enable you to become a more efficient communicator because you will be accurate and genuine every time you utter a word or a statement to yourself. Instead of responding to a situation routinely, describing something unpleasant with the stubbornness of a limited belief system, you can describe it for what it really is, a new situation. This is called a communication strategy. In any event, you have these five components:

1.) Who I am

2.) What I believe

3.) What I am capable of

4.) What I do

5.) What the environment is

A negative communication strategy looks like this:

Example: I cannot get a date.

Who I am: I'm unattractive.

What I believe: I won't ever have a chance at romance.

What I am capable of: I will just have to accept loneliness.

What I do: When I went out with my group of friends in the past, it made it easier to approach potential dates.

What the environment is: If only someone would approach me, I wouldn't have to worry about it anymore.

A positive communication strategy looks like this:

Example: I must get a date.

Who I am: I am unique and beautiful.

What I believe: There is someone I will meet with whom I am compatible.

What I am capable of: Every moment is an opportunity for meeting others, so I will be confident and open to those around me.

What I do: I will try what has worked before, going out with my group of friends and approaching potential dates. I will plan an outing this Friday!

What the environment is: A relaxing place full of potential friends and love interests and one in which I do not fear rejection.

You must be careful when you are communicating to yourself, because the way you communicate will input beliefs into both your conscious and your unconscious mind and obviously affect everything you feel and do. Remember that your unconscious mind cannot process negatives. It perceives things as positive thought. If you say, "I don't want to lose," the unconscious mind only focuses on the word "lose." Since the unconscious mind does not process negatives, the sentence becomes, "I want to lose." This is why it is important to state your goals positively. In order to direct the unconscious mind, you need to open up communication channels between your conscious and your unconscious mind. You can develop this rapport by finding quiet time for meditation or relaxation and examining the memories presented to you by your unconscious mind.

In 1957, the Penfield study indicated that all our experiences are recorded faithfully in memory.[4] While she was
awake, a woman's brain was stimulated with an electrode, and
Penfield discovered that the woman was able to vividly recall
the details of a childhood party in minute detail. The storage
and organization of these memories is the responsibility of the
unconscious mind. One function of the unconscious mind is
to repress memories with unresolved negative emotions.

The unconscious mind will keep you on the straight and
narrow path of whatever morality structure it has learned, even
if society later tries to uproot it and challenge your beliefs. A
terrorist will kill and destroy without qualms because his or
her moral code teaches them that they are a freedom fighter.
Therefore, they believe that they are actually being a moral
person in fighting against a criminal society. A gang member
may kill to protect the honor of his gang without feeling any
guilt, because he has learned that gang honor is more important than the Christian commandment "Thou shalt not kill,"
or the law of the land which makes murder illegal. If, however,
your unconscious decides that you deserve to be punished,
then you will be wracked with guilt and exhibit behaviors
designed to punish yourself, even though there may be no laws

---

4   Time Life Books, 1991, 76.

to incriminate you. What your unconscious discerns as "bad" will be convincing enough for you.

Your communication strategy is key because you can input into your conscious and unconscious mind a variety of empowering beliefs and statements about yourself and about the world in general. So talk to yourself. Be supportive. Be friendly. Be loving. The most feared critic in your life is yourself, so why not give yourself a damn good review!

Chapter Six: Passion

"Only passions, great passions, can elevate the soul to great things."

—*Denis Diderot*

Passion. Just the sound of this word will rouse in your mind a variety of desirable associations from your internal library of favorite emotions. Passion is Love. Passion is Excitement. Passion is Enthusiasm. Passion is whole-heartedly the underlying factor for why we are alive. We are born as a clean slate, taught this, taught that, we take, we contemplate, we believe, we decide, we respond, and we function. Usually while still young and confident with the possibility of what seems to be this never ending stretch of time laying ahead of us, we discover the first inklings of our passion, what we know we want to do with our lives. We may go to a screening of a huge, action-packed blockbuster or see opera singers singing their souls out on stage. We might meet a businessman or businesswoman, briefcase toting, charismatic, and powerful or see an exhibit that gets our heartbeat thumping at an unusual beat. We might be touched by a doctor's powerful healing or come across a book that rattles our bones and turns our world upside down. And we will think to ourselves, "Yes, this is what I want to do with my life. I want to be a part of this." So maybe we discover it later. Perhaps we are in our twenties, having not had much exposure to anything really moving, having just took a trip away from home, away from patterns, away from comfort, and just entering a big city with options, culture, new ideas, and new opportunities, and we find it there. Maybe we're in our thirties. Forties.

Passion has nothing to do with age. Having a cause, whether it involves making money or helping others, nurturing a family, or researching a subject, is available to any man or woman, every parent or child, every person who is alive and in touch with the world and ready to make an impact. Are *you* ready? You've heard clichés like, "I was born ready," and "Carpe Diem," or slogans like "Just do it," reminding you of the core human truth that life is short, so do something with it. And if you're going to do something with it, do what you're passionate about. And if you're going to do something passionate, then you're living your dream, and you can be assured that all other things will kindly fall into place ... it's quite difficult to be unhappy when you wake up every morning and your life is filled with something meaningful of your choosing.

To find your passion or rediscover it, you must know your driving force. Your driving force is was provokes you, what fuels you, what gets you going and keeps you at it. It is made up of your motivation, your plans and strategies, your actions, and your results. As beautiful as passion is, it is nothing but a dreamy thought in your mind, as isolated as a Da Vinci painting on an expensive museum wall if you don't use your driving force to develop it in your life. Don't let passion be a mere idea. Do something with it!

You may ask yourself a series of questions to find your motivation. First and foremost, what do you define as success? This definition might change every time you ask yourself. You'll have internal battles about whether or not you are using your limiting belief system to answer it, or whether or not you should answer it selfishly, or whether or not your idea of success is empowering enough. Look inwardly and you will remember. Then ask yourself, what drives you to be a successful human being? What goals do you want to accomplish? What makes you excited about being alive? What do you dislike about your life? What are you willing to do to arrive at success?

Once you understand your motivations and what you inherently want, you must create your plan to attain it. To create a plan, you must list all the strategies you'd be willing to use. With this list, provide necessary phone numbers and other paperwork that will help you execute your plan. Prepare yourself for action.

The key, most important, most deliberate step is of course to take action. On the day of action, on the day that you take your first step of what may be a 100 to 1,000 to 10,000-step journey, begin your day with gratitude. Write down or say aloud 10 things for which you are grateful. It would be beneficial if you started to make a habit of doing this every day since every day is simply another step along the path of your journey. Starting your day off with gratitude starts your day off with hope. Your mindset will be in a positive place and you will automatically continue to seek out more things for which you can be grateful, i.e. your accomplishments. Do daily affirmations and incantations such as, "I am capable," and "I am an amazing person." Take massive action on your plan, meaning if you want to go back to college and earn your degree, make a phone call and enroll. Lastly, stick to your strategies! They will only work if you follow through. The last step to evolving your driving force into your passion is to keep track of each result of every strategic action. If something isn't working or delivering results, change your approach. Be consistent. Just remember sometimes it takes time to get the results, after all Rome was not built in one day.

It cannot be stressed enough how exceedingly important it is to actually have goals. If you don't have goals and especially ones that derive from your passion, you will go through life blindly, accomplishing not much. You might dream a lot, you might experience occasional moments of good fortune, but you will never be as fulfilled as the person who decided to have something he or she wanted, developed a plan of acquiring, and then basked in his or her accomplishment. To bask in accomplishment is one of the most rewarding experiences in life. Do you know what the smell and taste and heat of accomplishment is? Find out. Look inwardly and ask yourself what you want most. Make a list of short and long-term goals. Separate them into three categories: business, personal, and financial. Ask yourself the following questions:

1.) What position am I in?

2.) What position do I want to be in?

3.) What are things I want to experience in life?

4.) How much vacation time do I want?

5.) How much money do I want to make?

6.) How much money do I want to save?

Keep in mind the cause and effect patterns that take place while achieving your goals. For each one, there should be an action, and for every action, there is a reaction. Most people wait for things to happen in their lives, hoping someday they will have everything they ever dreamed of. To hope is not enough. Most people die without having everything they dreamed of, thinking an extravagant life was meant only for the television screen or glossy magazine covers. You cannot wait for things to happen. You have to put a cause in motion that will create an effect in your life that you are happy with. Start structuring your experiences into cause/effect patterns.

1.) The more you (x), the more you (y)

2.) The less you (x), the more you (y)

3.) The more you (x), the fewer you (y)

4.) The less you (x), the less you (y)

The more you practice tennis, the more balls you hit. The less you brush your teeth, the more cavities you get. The more you become organized, the fewer hours you need to work. The less you ask, the less you learn. Every action gets a reaction, if you like the reaction, repeat the action, if it's not so hot, do something else. Although much of this may sound elementary, most of the complexity in our lives stems from being unable to follow basic, fundamental truths such as this. Every cause has an effect. Pay attention.

Of course the only way to lucratively develop your goals passionately is to feel worthy of them. And the only way you will feel worthy day in and day out, unaffected by negative images, unresponsive to limiting thoughts, is by consistently reinforcing a positive mindset. This can be prompted every morning with your affirmations and lists of gratitude, but you must be able to sustain this mindset throughout your day to accomplish positive tasks. The power of your thoughts is something that most people simply don't understand. Your thoughts are like a steering wheel in a car that drives in NASCAR. Your thoughts become something. They have results. There have been studies done that have confirmed that a positive thought will actually increase the helper cells in your immune systems. Which means if you had more of them, you would be less likely to get sick. (Cause and effect affirmation: "The more positive thoughts I have, the less likely I am to get sick.") Studies also confirmed that when you have a negative thought, you actually lose your helper cells in your immune system. This is obviously an adverse result.

Most of us start our day in a negative mindset. You might immediately flip on the local news upon waking and be subjected to a parade of depressing news stories. You might even end your day the same way, with the nightly news showcasing just as much bad news as you found in the morning. Then you wonder why you're not in a positive mindset. With what are you bombarding your mind? A lot of people ask me, "Sam, how can I stay positive when I have so many problems?" The way you can start each day, as previously suggested, is to write down 5 to 10 things for which you are grateful. When you write this down, when you actively pursue positive things, your mind and your day have no other choice but to begin positively. What are five things for which you are grateful?

_____

_____

_____

_____

_____

Many people know of Steve Irwin, the Crocodile Hunter. He was an Australian wildlife expert and television personality. He achieved worldwide fame from his television show "The Crocodile Hunter," in which he exhibited unfaltering enthusiasm in the face of the most dangerous animals on earth. Through Irwin's enthusiasm, you could see his passion. It was obvious and gleaming through his eyes, his words, and the overall energy he emitted. That is why he was so successful. The problem most people have is that they don't want to show enthusiasm, so they mask it from themselves just as often as they mask it from others. Why? They are worried what people will say about them if they are too enthusiastic. They feel that they might find rejection through their enthusiasm since the majority of times they find acceptance with others is when they're having a bad day or experiencing some kind of drama. When you are experiencing drama, people will always approach you to ask how you are doing and ask you out for a drink or lunch to go talk about it. The truth is that when your friends or co-workers listen to your problems, most of them are thinking, "Thank God this is not happening to me. My life is so much better theirs." They take you out and listen to you complain so they can feel better about themselves. Who do you surround yourself with?

Not many years ago, a study was conducted to discover why so many people showed up at funerals for people they had not seen for over 10 years. If they truly cared about the person, they would have visited with this person and been a part of his or her life while they were still alive. However, along the same lines of friends taking you out to feel better about themselves, the studies found that when most people are at funerals, they are repeating to themselves over and over again: "Life is so precious. I should slow down and cherish it more." The funeral becomes a moment for reflection, a somewhat meditative practice, where the attendee becomes more saturated in himself than the memory of the person who has died.

Are these images of people you want to be like or be surrounded by? These people will get you nowhere. Many times when we bump into acquaintances and friends and we're asked how we are doing, we respond with mediocre, automatic answers. We say, "Fine," or "Okay," or "So, so." What is that? Even when things are going really well in our lives, like we've just had a baby, or we've gotten a promotion, or we're finally taking control of our health, we still give the same automatic answers. We have been conditioned to not celebrate our wins. Yet, when some of us go to a football game or boxing match, we get excited, jump out of our seats, and exclaim to everyone, "Yes! We did it!!! We won!!!" You did what? You won what? You simply bought a ticket, ate some nachos, and observed the victories of other people. The only people that truly benefit from sporting wins, unless you have some placed bet, are the football players or the boxers themselves. If you simply take that same enthusiasm and apply it in your work and personal life, you can transport yourself and your levels of fulfillment to phenomenal heights. Celebrate your own wins! Nobody is in the sidelines, eating nachos, watching you. But you are always present in your own life, watching and judging every move you make. Start counting your victories.

I mentioned before the concept of daily affirmations. They put you in a positive mindset and should be combined with making gratitude lists to obtain optimum results. Making affirmations is a valuable technique to get you in the zone of being positive and pumped up. For example, when we lose our keys, most of us say to ourselves over and over, "I don't know where I put my keys, I don't know where I put my keys, I don't know where I put my keys." We keep saying this as we keep looking and only until we calm down and practically give up do we find our keys in the original spot we first thought to look. The reason that we did not see the keys in the original spot is because we kept telling ourselves that we couldn't see keys. Our eyes believed us. This is an example of a negative affirmation.

In the same sense, you can get your eyes and your bodies and your brains to believe positive things if you stress positive affirmations enough times. Muhammad Ali used to always say before a fight, "I am the greatest, I am the greatest, I am the greatest." Many people recognize Ali and he certainly recognized himself as the greatest boxer who ever lived. He simply reinforced the idea that he was great to become great. It works every time, guaranteed. Imagine you saying powerful affirmations every morning. What could you accomplish in your ordinary day? Say these aloud as you read them:

1.) I am the best.

2.) I attract positive people and things into my life.

3.) Good things happen to me every day.

4.) I am a positive thinker.

5.) I trust myself.

6.) I believe in myself.

7.) I know I can do it.

8.) I can easily make decisions.

9.) I have complete control over my future.

10.) I am not attached to the outcome.

11.) I am 100 percent committed to my success.

12.) My thoughts are extremely powerful.

13.) I am alive, excited, and full of energy.

14.) I am already successful in my mind.

15.) I am grateful for everything in my life.

Start off each day with 5-10 things you are grateful for and by practicing your affirmations and note any changes that occur. You will notice a big difference in your mindset and energy level. More people will be attracted to you and they will want to be part of your energy. Allow them. When you say your affirmations, don't just say them with a normal voice. Speak with incredible enthusiasm so that your ears will believe you. Use your whole body so that your brain isn't just the one focusing, but so is your whole being. You will breathe differently. You will think differently. You will live differently.

PART TWO:
ACT DIFFERENT

CHAPTER SEVEN: KNOCK, KNOCK, KNOCKIN' ON GREATNESS'S DOOR

"Be not afraid of greatness: some men are born great, some achieve greatness and some have greatness thrust upon them."

—William Shakespeare from 'Twelfth Night'

Models. No longer must you associate this word with half-starved girls in $30,000 gowns strutting down the catwalk during Paris' Fashion Week. In Neuro-linguistic Programming, models are the individuals who have achieved greatness or excellence in areas we desire, leaving footsteps deep enough for us to fill and follow. Simply by leading their successful lives, models leave maps to their success in their vision, language, physiology, and overall belief systems. As NLPers, we are able to duplicate their successes in less time simply by avoiding their mistakes and modeling the correct decisions they have made which delivered them to their success. We are then able to identically reproduce their attractive results.

Have you ever wondered what separates highly successful people from the rest of the pack? Take multibillionaire Donald Trump. Not only does he love his job, but he consistently produces extraordinary results and attracts teams of people who love to work for him. This is the same story for Oprah Winfrey and Richard Branson, the CEO of the Virgin companies. Take a look at Mahatma Gandhi and Mother Teresa. There are various names that come to mind. Who are your favorite models?

What makes these people different? What separates them from the Average Joe? What separates them from you? Some years of research revealed that all individuals who consistently produce extraordinary results, regardless of the field, share some fundamental characteristics, attitudes, tools and strategies that make them stand out. And the most exciting thing about this discovery is that these characteristics are entirely duplicable. Sometimes when we look at these achievers, we place them on an unreachable pedestal and assume they are so much more advanced than us and that their achievements are impossible for us to attain. This is a limiting belief.

The first component of a model that must be duplicated, regardless of their expertise, is their vision. Your vision is the most critical aspect of your success. It is your final destination, your place of arrival. Your vision is the foundation upon which you build your family, your business, your dreams, and your life. Take the construction of great buildings. Someone imagined these buildings before any plans were drawn. Then the drawings of these buildings were created, followed by blueprints for construction. Once these were created, builders were able to take their tools and start building. When you build a house, you have a plan before you start building. The same applies to your life. Create a vision and a plan and start building. The end result is a reflection of your creative mind.

Take the time to create the vision for your ideal life. If it takes you more time than you thought, it is a good sign. It means your creative mind is really working. During the process, ask yourself questions. What does my ideal house look like? How many cars do I have? How many goals do I achieve every day, every week, every month, every year? Who are my loved ones? What aspects of my life do I spend the majority of my day on? How much money am I generating every month, every year? Who are my business partners? Do I have employees? How many? Who are my mentors? Who are my models? Who has succeeded in areas that are important to me? Read their biographies. Watch them being interviewed on the news. If you know them personally, find out what their vision is! What drove them to success? What do they believe? The great thing about reading books written by people like Albert Einstein or Hilary Clinton or whomever you admire most, is it will put you in a similar state of mind as theirs. You will begin to match their internal representations and perhaps begin to behave like them. That is the effects of studying models.

Of course, you don't always have to look to outlandish celebrity figures for doses of inspiration. You could model people who are close to you as well. Someone ordinary like your next-door neighbor might have qualities that you admire and wish to have. Find out what inspires him or her and what keeps them focused on achieving the things you admire most about them. Modeling someone's qualities or successes are simple ways to turn negative feelings of jealousy into productive experiences for learning a new way. What do you do and how can I learn? Just ask.

The list of questions is endless and it should be. There should always be a new question on developing your vision and bettering yourself. The more details you can fit into your image, the sooner you will achieve what you want. In my mind, a life without a vision is like a ship without a rudder, at the mercy of the elements. It is sure to arrive somewhere, but not necessarily where the captain would like it to arrive. The same applies to parenting. If you want to raise responsible, self-disciplined children, you must have a clear vision of the desired end result of your efforts. Every time you interact with your children, you must behave in a fashion that works toward the desired end result. You must plan a garden before you plant it. If you are to give a speech, you must know the goal you want to accomplish and the content before you write it on paper and finally present it. Everything starts with a vision. What is yours?

If you do not have a vision, by default you are allowing other people and circumstances to determine your reality and run your life. You conduct your life in a reactive mode, imprisoned by other people's expectations. You are the architect of your reality. Take charge NOW!

I would like to share the strategy I use to develop my vision. It works for me and it will work for you, just as it has worked for countless of other successful people. Create a vision board. Buy a display board at any office supply store. Put it up in a very visible place and glue onto it physical images of everything you want in your life. That's right. If you imagine having a particular home, find a picture of such a home, cut it out and place it upon your board. I found mine in Robb's Report. I particularly enjoy this publication as it contains images of several things I would like to have. One of my big dreams is to own a yacht. I have found a picture of exactly the kind I want and I have it on my vision board. I look at it every day and I know one day I will own such a boat. Whatever you desire, you put it up on your board. When you start doing this exercise, at times you may notice certain uncomfortable feelings. During those times, ask yourself: "Whose limitation am I allowing to influence my dreams?" I realized very quickly that I was unconsciously influenced by the beliefs held by my family. I grew up in an environment where the predominant belief was that only years of hard work could generate financial rewards. Young people like me were not supposed to have a lot of money, and certainly not earn it very quickly. I was not supposed to dream about cars, mansions, huge offices, or fat bank accounts. In fact, having those things would mean I did something dishonest or unlawful. So when I created my first vision board and placed a picture of a Ferrari on it, I felt guilty. I was stepping outside of my comfort zone, threatening the belief system I was raised in. I did it anyway and now that picture has become a reality.

Allow your positive thoughts to become positive results. Thoughts are units of energy that influence the overall energy field existing around us, shaping our lives. Positive, structured thoughts positively impact our reality. Didn't you notice that successful people always think about possibilities? They have the courage to dream really big. They see opportunities everywhere. Their vision is limitless. "The sky is the limit," as cliché as that sounds, is their motto. And guess what? Even the sky is no longer a limit. Think Neil Armstrong. When Walt Disney created his dream, he envisioned himself changing the world by bringing magic into the lives of children. He didn't know how he would do it. He just knew that he would. And he did.

All great inventions start with an idea. The thought turns into an action. Actions create reality. I now have five vision boards. I have fun dreaming up my future. My kids are little but they also have fun playing with ideas. They are excited when they see their Dad putting pretty pictures on his board. Just recently my oldest child asked me to buy for her her own vision board. She said she wanted to put a picture of shoes that she wanted on it, so that by Christmas she would have them. Guess what she received as a Christmas present? Start today with your dream. Children have limitless imaginations. Take their example and model it. It all starts in your head.

Have fun! Think about some other models that have achieved desirable results and imagine what their vision was. Consider Warren Buffett.

When a reporter asked Warren Buffett, an American investor, businessman, and philanthropist and one of the richest men on this planet, "what he attributed his success to," Warren responded with a story.

He said that when Bobby Fischer, the American chess player, was playing chess against a Russian player, a big debate ensued about whether a human being could beat a computer at chess. All the articles coming out on the question adamantly said that a human being could not beat a computer because a computer has the ability to contemplate every infinitesimal possibility and choose the best move to win the game. But what they found was just the opposite—a human being could not only tie a computer, but could sometimes beat it through a process of what Buffett called "selective grouping." Selective grouping is the internal process by which humans can automatically discount 90 percent of possibilities without ever having to consider them fully, so that they can focus their attention on the remaining 10 percent of possible moves that would make the greatest strategic impact. "If you want to know what makes our overwhelming success," Buffett responded, "It's been selective grouping. It's what we focus on. And equally important, it's what we choose not to focus on."

The same applies to your life. What you focus on determines your results. When you focus on what you don't want, you also produce results, but only ones that are opposite to those you wanted to produce. Just think about it. If you focus on making more money for instance, you create strategies to make more money and consequently you make more money. If you focus on how hard it will be to make more money, you will inevitably experience hardship. When you realize that your focus determines your results, you will also become a better time manager. You will ask yourself the question, "Where am I spending the most of my time?"

Another useful tactic to acquiring your vision besides having a vision board is to keep a dream diary. Look at your life like a filled-up, busy day planner. You enter appointments faithfully but sometimes you forget and miss out. Look at your unrealized dreams as those appointments you forgot to write down. You didn't forget to buy bread and eggs. You didn't forget to take the lower pay though you knew you deserved more. You didn't forget to settle on the first offer. You did forget to buy the house you really wanted, or ask for the higher pay, or work harder and purposefully toward the better career. Why did you forget these things? By not writing them down, by not stressing the importance of them in your mind, you consequently made these things unimportant so unrealized. Just as you would buy another day planner or calendar for you always busy life, buy a dream diary for the life you wish you had. When you write down a dream or goal, consider the desired outcome of each and keep your word that you will make the dream come true just as you would be sure to show up for an appointment. Make sure there is a clear date and set up a plan for the following week that will help you see clearly just how this will get done. And it will.

Perception and Vision

What you experience in your life and your business is determined by how you perceive the information you are constantly bombarded with. Your perceptual filters help you process information, and decide what you concentrate on. To illustrate this point, imagine you are going to buy a new car. You know you like a particular brand and color. Let's say it is a BMW, M3 Series, cobalt blue. As you contemplate the purchase of this car, you are more likely going to notice such a car on the highway. The likelihood of you paying attention to a cobalt blue BMW, M3 is much higher than of you noticing a red Honda Civic. Also, once you decided to buy that car, you will pay attention to the strategies of how to buy it. You will make a decision to lease it or to finance it, or to buy it straight out. You will be focused on getting that car.

Your brain works very much like the World Wide Web. When you go to Google and search for a specific phrase, you will immediately be presented with all the possible matches for the criteria you entered. All the other irrelevant pages are left out. The search engine translated your request and delivered possible solutions to you based on what you asked for.

Your world takes on the form that you recognize only after it has passed through your perception filters. It is important to realize that what information is processed and what information is missed depends entirely on the individual. For example, a business tycoon may never notice a billboard for a men's bodybuilding competition. People starving in Africa may never be inclined to read a Wall Street Journal, and professional bodybuilders may never pay attention to today's ocean tides. The only thing that determines your concept of reality and your outcomes in life is what you pay attention to. Your focus creates what is real for you in your world. By changing your focus, you can change your reality and your outcomes.

Let's recap the essence of one of the most powerful books on focus that I have ever read, "Man's Search for Meaning" by Viktor Frankl. Dr. Frankl was a survivor of four different death camps during the Nazi occupation. As a neurologist and psychiatrist, Dr. Frankl was able to examine the difference between those who pushed to survive, and those who were crushed by their circumstances and died. Most of Dr. Frankl's family, including his wife, brother and parents were among those who died. He also lost most of his friends.

The only difference between those who survived and those who died, he said, was that those who lived focused on a different outcome. They found a way to ascribe a different purpose or meaning to their abhorrent circumstances. They found a larger vision and saw their current circumstances as being just the thing that would allow them to gain extraordinary strength and invincibility. Some people were committed to sharing their story with others so that the horrors of the Holocaust would never occur again. Some experienced a state of enlightenment and wanted to share their spirituality with others to make the world a better place. By believing something good would come from their experience, they were able to survive. By changing your focus, you can change your experiences. In life and death situations, changing your focus may be the determining factor that decides your survival. If you focus on what you want, you will gather the tools to achieve it. You will also discover people showing up on your path who will assist you in achieving your goals. I am not sure how this works, but I am certain that it does. The universe has a mysterious way of responding to powerful wishes and generating opportunities congruent with clear visions. I consistently observe this phenomenon in my personal and professional life. When I focus on what I want, things happen and opportunities arise when I'm least expecting them.

Although most of us will never experience any atrocity even close to the Holocaust, the lesson is clear and applicable to all experiences throughout your life, large or small. You can figure out anyone's mental syntax by looking for things you weren't seeing before and asking questions you didn't think to ask before. People are communicating their vision to you every day, but it's up to you to decide whose vision you want to learn from and adapt as your own. People will communicate with you through their body language, their tone, and of course through their choice of words. Once you learn to adhere to the visions of the masters, you will able to use their techniques to not only dream big, but to also live big. When you're being a moved by someone extraordinary, when you're in the essence of greatness, will you react or will you act? Three, Two, One … ACTION!

Chapter Eight:
More than Meets the
Mind

"I want all my senses engaged. Let me absorb the world's variety and uniqueness."

—*Maya Angelou*

You can destroy limiting internal maps and replace them with maps to success based on the techniques provided by masters of excellence. In the first part of this book we learned that our minds are made up mostly of limiting belief systems and a distortion of reality. We learned that all versions of our reality are distorted since we only know what we perceive. But we also learned that by studying the ones who have achieved greatness, our distortions could lead to just as uplifting and extraordinary consequences as theirs. Our distortions can lead to realms of unfolding possibility in which we achieve all the dreams of our wildest imaginations. We know that we must change our minds, that we must begin thinking positively, and only until we do that will we be able to successfully interact with others and learn to negotiate getting what we want from other people and from the world. We know we must change our minds, but how exactly do we do that? Making affirmations is a good start. Developing a positive vision is even better. But let's travel into your brains, the most complex computer system that has ever existed, and learn how to use your equipment so that you may become the master of yourself. Only until you are the master of your mind, will you be a master in the world. Look within.

We know that those who have achieved excellence in the world achieved excellence in their minds first and foremost. First let's break down the term NLP, the science that lends itself to us most promisingly as we start to understand the functions of our minds.

Neuro is about your neurological system. NLP is based on premise that we experience the world through our senses and translate this sensory information into thought processes, both conscious and unconscious. Thought processes are what activate the neurological system, affecting our bodies, emotions, and behavior.

Linguistic refers to the way human beings use language to make sense of our world, capturing and conceptualizing experience, and then communicating in our own separate ways this experience to others. In NLP, linguistics is the study of how the words you speak influence your experience.

Programming is based on learning theory and addresses how we code or internally represent our experience to ourselves. Your own programming consists of your internal processes and thinking patterns that you use to make decisions, solve problems, learn, decode, and get results. NLP shows people how to redefine their experiences and organize their internal talk and programming so that they can achieve outcomes they desire most.

Human beings experience the world they live in through the primary modalities of the five senses: seeing, hearing, feeling, smelling, and tasting. The sensory modalities by which people encode, organize, store, and attach meaning to perceptual input are referred to as representational systems. As sensory input is internally processed (re-represented), it is translated into corresponding sensory representations (or maps) that constitute a likeness to the original perceptual block. So, again, reality and our perceptions of reality are not ever the same. The map is not the territory!

We use preferred representational systems to store information in different ways. Let's imagine that there was an armed robbery on a late Tuesday afternoon and a group of people witnessed it. Each person would have a different view of what happened. This is because each of us processes information in our brain a different way. The three major representation systems are the visual, the auditory and the kinesthetic.

The visual preference may mean that you see clearly, keep your eye on things, and take a long-term view. You may enjoy visual images, watching sports, symbols, design, math and chemistry. You may have an attractively designed environment. The witness of the above robbery who owned a visual preference might have noticed the clothes the thief was wearing, the color of his skin, or in which direction he ran.

The auditory preference may mean that you are easily tuned into new idea, maintain harmonious relationships, and often sound people out. You may enjoy music, drama, writing, speaking, and literature. You may often manage the sound levels in your environments. The witness with the auditory preference would have noticed the crash of windows, the screech of the car, the shouts of other witnesses or victims of the crime.

The kinesthetic preference may mean you are drawn to the latest trends; you are concerned with balance and with holding onto your preset notions of reality. You may enjoy contact sports, athletics, climbing, working with materials, electronics and manufacturing. You may need to have a highly comfortable environment at all times. The witness with a kinesthetic preference would have noticed what time of day it was by how warm it felt and the vibrations of a speeding car taking off in a particular direction.

People have a tremendous wealth of sensory information available to them in all systems at any given amount of time. Imagine yourself in as normal a place as your living room. Even with the windows shut, you might be able to hear cars driving outside, birds chirping, perhaps people's voices as they speak to each other. Maybe there is a slam of a car door. Perhaps the wind is whirring away. Then of course, you've got the television turned on and not only do you hear the characters chatting on screen, maybe you hear the static of having the power turned on, or maybe the background music is tugging at your emotions to shift in a particular way. Then again, these are only sounds. There might be more coming from other rooms, not to mention your own breathing and heartbeat, stomach rumbling and sniffling. Add all these sounds to as many visual particles your brain is being subjected to, and how many sensations your body is feeling, and you have yourself an abundance of sensory information.

Sensory information is filtered in various ways by the Central Nervous System, thereby allowing a limited amount of sensory information into conscious awareness at any one time. This filtering mechanism screens perceptual input with a set of systematic functions: deletion, distortion, and generalization. Without these neurological filters, people would be overwhelmed by a constant bombardment of irrelevant information. These modeling processes make it possible for human beings to maintain coherent models of their experience. You can effectively tune out the car slams and children crying outside and the constant thump-thump of your heartbeat, just as you can effectively tune out the negative images constantly available for you to seize from your environment and from those already established in your brain. Before you are able to identify these filters in action to determine what people are REALLY saying behind their words and phrases, you must find out what you are deleting, distorting, and generalizing yourself. The best way to find this out is to discover what representational system you prefer. Answer the following statements:

1.) I make major decisions based on:

   a.) What looks good to me

   b.) My gut feeling

   c.) Which options sound best

2.) How do you know that the presentation was valuable to you?

   a.) I felt the real issues

   b.) The key points were clearly illustrated

   c.) The points sounded great

3.) People know if I am having a good or bad day by:

   a.) The way I dress and look

   b.) The thoughts and feelings I share

   c.) The tone of my voice

4.) If I have a disagreement, I am most influenced by:

   a.) The sound of the other person's voice

   b.) How they look at me

   c.) Connecting with their feelings

5.) I am very aware of:

    a.) The sounds and noises around me

    b.) The touch of different clothes on my body

    c.) The colors and shapes in my surroundings

Which preference was most dominant? Circle the letter you chose and corresponding representational system. (V=Visual preference, A=Auditory preference, K=Kinesthetic preference)

1.) a= V, b= K, c= A

2.) a= K, b= V, c= A

3.) a= V, b= K, c= A

4.) a= A, b= V, c= K

5.) a= A, b= K, c= V

Everything in our perception of the world is filtered through our senses and especially what representational systems we prefer. If we are a more visually stimulated person, we'd notice more about a person's features and physiology, how they dress and move and hold themselves more than what they are saying to us or how they feel in embrace. In memory, we would hold onto specific places as far as physical features, saying things like, "Oh my house was so small when I was a child, it was often very dark …" and go on to describe the furnishings and wall fixtures. You would vividly remember the experience in terms of who was there, what was involved, the objects and colors and placement of things associated to your feelings about them. Your emotions are then most anchored in these features and to access them, you would simply have to imagine in your mind these visual details.

If someone produces a result that we would like to model, we need to know more than the fact that he pictured something in his mind or said something to himself. We need sharper tools to really access what's happening in his mind. This is where submodalities come into play. Submodalities are the precise amount of factors or ingredients needed in order to attain a specific result. In order to understand and control a visual experience, we need to know everything about it. We need to know if it's dark or bright, if it's colorful or black and white, if it's moving or still. If we're trying to process an auditory experience, we must know how loud it is or if it is near or far. The same goes for a kinesthetic experience. Is it soft or hard? Sharp or smooth?

Another distinction is determining whether an image is associated or disassociated. An associated image is one that you experience as if you were actually there. You see it with your own eyes, and you hear it and feel it, as if you had been transported there in your own body. A disassociated image is one you experience as if you were watching from outside of yourself. If you visualize a disassociated image of yourself, it's like you are watching a movie of yourself. Below is a checklist of possible submodalities you would use when describing an experience. This will help you understand of what exactly your perception is composed:

SUBMODALITIES

Visual	Size
	Motion/Still
	Distance
	Location
	Bright/Dim
	Shape
	Number of Images
	Framed/Unframed
	Color/Black & White
	Associated/Disassociated
	Focused/Unfocused
	3D/Flat

Auditory	Number of Sounds
	Volume
	Tone
	Tempo
	Pitch
	Pace
	Direction
	Intensity
	Distance
	Location
	Harmony
	Stereo
	Rhythm
Kinesthetic	Location in Body
	Breathing Rate
	Pulse Rate
	Pressure
	Tactile Sensations
	Direction
	Intensity
	Weight
	Scope
	Movement

For Pain	Tingling
	Hot-Cold
	Muscle Tension
	Sharp-Dull
	Pressure
	Duration
	Intermittent (such as throbbing)
	Location

Pause for a moment and remember a recent pleasant experience you've had. Really belong to the experience and imagine yourself inside of it. See what you saw through your eyes, the images, colors, brightness, all the necessary submodalities. Hear what you heard, the sounds, voices, tempo, etc. Feel what you felt at that particular time, emotions, temperature, all contributing factors. Now separate yourself from your body and situation, but don't go too far, imagine that you are watching yourself in the experience, as if you were on a huge movie screen. Note the differences in your feelings. In which were the feelings more intense? Was it in the first example or in the second? The difference between these is that the first is an associated experience and the second is a disassociated experience.

You can use associated and disassociated experiences and other submodality distinctions to drastically change your experience in life. Most of our limiting beliefs and negative memories are rooted in these submodalities, the sounds of your past experiences, or the vividness of how things felt or appeared in a most uncomfortable situation. In order for you to be able to tap into a memory and tweak it so that you can change its emotion and effect on your life, you will have to use all three representational systems and perform what is called a "reprogramming" of the brain. Just as a movie director can change the effects his movie has on an audience, you can change the effect that any experience has had on you. A director can change the camera angle, the type and volume of music, the speed and movement of each scene, thus creating the emotional states of his audience. You can direct your brain in the same way to generate any state or behavior that supports your highest goals or needs.

Consider the pleasant memory you recalled a moment ago. Close your eyes, relax, and think of it and all the components that made it real. Consider the submodalities that were most vivid in the experience. Now take that image and make it brighter and brighter. As the image brightens, be aware of how your state changes. Now take the image and bring it closer to you. Next step is to make it bigger. What happens to your emotions as you manipulate the image? The intensity of the experience should change as well and your feelings will start to become powerful toward it, reframing the experience as one that was truly meaningful and powerful. You will associate a higher level of joy with it.

If you prefer an auditory representational system, the intensity of your pleasant experience would be further enhanced if you simply raised the volume of the voices or sounds of those involved. Put more rhythm and bass into the experience. Do the same with kinesthetic submodalities. Some representational systems work better than others. Your pleasant experience might not seem so pleasant after you start altering its auditory submodalities so choose whichever system would work best for you.

Once you become aware of the representational systems, then your life can be affected in many enriching ways. For instance, you can start developing your goals so that they are more realistic for yourself. Use all your senses! Think of the way your goals will look, sound, and feel once they are achieved in your life. If you want to truly motivate others or yourself, step out of your comfort zone (if you prefer visuals) of imagining yourself in your brand new house with high ceilings and French doors and crown molding. Imagine the sounds of a football game resonating from the plasma TV;

imagine the splashing from the pool in the backyard and the heat of your very own sauna too.

You can use your senses to influence a business meeting, training session, or presentation. Remember that when you're speaking to a large group of people, every one of those people has his or her own way of processing information, and you don't know what that is. You need to ensure that you connect with every person's chosen representational system by presenting your information with a variety of media. Use visual aids with pictures, or auditory samples with interviews or songs and perhaps models people can pass around and touch so that you appeal to all senses.

In the same sense, you can apply the variety of aids with your children, whether you are a parent or teacher or big sister or uncle. If you have contact with children, find out which representational system works best with them. Many times children are incorrectly labeled as "slow" simply because their teacher's or parent's learning style is different from theirs. Keep that in mind the next time you want to share a story or play a game or teach something new to a child you know.

Just remember to have fun with your senses! An entertaining practice of mine is picking sense themes for each day. This is a way for me to learn how to master my senses, becoming appreciative of each one of them. For instance, I could name tomorrow a visual day, where I will make a point of turning off music around me and focus only on the sights, shapes, and pictures of what's around me. A touch day can be especially interesting, when you pay close attention to textures and weight of things around you and check in with your feelings at regular points in the day. Notice how habits will start to break up and diminish when you pay close attention to a particular sense and then change it up for another. You will start to be more present and appreciate every minute of your day and how much is living inside each one.

Chapter Nine:
Architecting Thought

"Don't find fault, find a remedy."

—Henry Ford

Now we are going to use the most effective tools, your senses, to reprogram the viruses or bugs in your brain's software. You don't have to leave your home or office and head to the electronics store. You don't have to search through the phonebook for a brain surgeon who will implant new brain mass and new thoughts. Your senses are yours and are readily available to assist you. The only thing that paralyzes them and keeps you in a state of powerless suspension is this big, overbearing blob of negative talk. Negative talk is one of the most insidious ways in which we block rapport with ourselves and sabotage success. It creates negative feelings, limiting belief systems, and obliterates our resources and creativity. A depressed or fearful person cannot fully access their potential and operates with a limited repertoire of abilities. I remember a friend of mine in high school who continually told himself that he couldn't perform well in mathematics. Even though he did his homework, practiced his exercises, and understood the material, on the examination days, he "forgot" almost everything and failed. His poor results did not reflect his skills. Finally, one day my friend admitted that he knew he would not do well on his test because his father told him he would not do well. And then he would be punished when this premonition came true. My friends' self-talking, based on his fear of punishment from his father had blocked his ability to express his skills, thus sabotaging his chances for admission to a good college.

Negative self-talk is a source of much misery in our lives. Fortunately, we can easily change it. One strategy for doing this, and a favorite of cognitive psychologists is to say STOP! If you say this faithfully whenever you start becoming aware of negative self-talk, your brain will force you to take a break and re-evaluate the situation.

Another efficient way to eliminating negative self-talk is to replace it with a positive self-talk which was the key point suggested in reciting daily affirmations or listing things for which you are grateful. When you catch yourself using negative language, say to yourself, "You are better than this. Yes, you can do it. You can get this result." You will start building a reflex response to your negative self-talk and linking a new neuro pathway for your thoughts to follow. To do this, you must pay attention to your feelings and become attuned to the internal dialogue you use when you talk to yourself.

Another very effective way to eradicate negative self-talk is by reframing. The first step is self-awareness. When confronted with adversity, some of us will say things like: "I'm not good at this," or "Nothing will work anyway," or "I'm not able to do it." We attribute the adversity to some inadequacy in ourselves and confirm our paralysis by telling ourselves that it applies to everything we attempt and that it will last forever. The foundation for a pessimistic world-view is thus firmly established, and the attribute is personal, permanent, and pervasive.

One way to get out of the pessimism is through appropriate attribution. I read a book, *Learned Optimism*, by Martin Seligman, which perhaps the greatest manual for combating a negative mindset. In his book, Martin recommends a frame that he calls the ABC model. "A" stands for adversity, an event that triggers the negative emotional state, "B" stands for a belief that is reflected in negative self-talk, and "C" is the consequence of this belief. Negative beliefs will erode any sense of personal power, leading to very predictable negative outcomes. Once you become aware of this pattern, Seligman suggests adding additional steps, "D" and "E" to the process. "D" stands for Disputation. "E" stands for Energizing. When we notice ourselves engaging in negative self-talk, we need to dispute the underlying belief. He suggests the following ways to dispute a debilitating belief.

1.) Marshall the evidence to the contrary. If you catch yourself saying, "I am not capable, I am not lucky, I am not successful," find evidence to disprove this belief. You may say to yourself, "I am capable, I succeeded at finishing college," or "I am lucky, I live in the best country in the world, I have a future ahead of me, and I am healthy." The more evidence you find to dispute the negative belief, the weaker the belief will become.

2.) Create an alternative to the belief. Find another explanation. Consider my friend in high school who failed his tests because he believed he had no skills. His results were not a direct reflection of his skills but of the mere belief itself.

3.) Determine the usefulness of the belief. Ask yourself, "How useful is this belief? Does it serve me? (Perhaps it helps me to be careful in situations I am not sure of.)

The last step in Seligman's process is "E," which stands for Energizing. When we are successful in disputing our negative beliefs, we feel energized and optimistic.

The Swish Pattern to Reframe a Negative Self-Image

Negative self-talk often results from a negative self-image. When we have a negative self-image, we can easily change it, just as we change channels on our television set. The technique of replacing a negative self-image with a positive self-image is called a Swish Pattern. This is how it works:

1.) Imagine yourself sitting in front of a television, with two channels on the screen at the same time, a large full size picture and a smaller picture in one of the corners of the bigger picture.

2.) Imagine yourself in a desired emotional state (happy, energetic, optimistic, powerful, resourceful, any positive state you want to access) and create a picture of this state. Imagine yourself being in that state, the way you look, the way you behave, the way you handle the situation at hand, the way you talk to people, etc.

3.) Insert the picture of the positive state into the smaller window of your mental screen. You can make the image still or it can be a set of moving pictures. Make the image brighter, the colors more vivid, and add any qualities that might make this image more attractive.

4.) Switch the images ("swish") so that the larger undesired state becomes small, and the smaller desired state becomes larger. You can make the picture of the undesired state black and white, or make it dim, or make it so dark that nothing can be seen. If the image has sounds associated with it, make the sounds sound like cartoon characters.

5.) Repeat the image switching several times until you can do it really quickly.

The objective of this exercise is to replace the negative image in your subconscious mind with a positive image. But the key to its success is by speed and repetition when you swap the two images. You can use this technique at anytime you wish to replace any negative image with a positive one.

If you simply cannot visualize the Swish Pattern, try the slingshot method instead. Hold a big, bright, loud picture in your mind of a behavior or trait you find undesirable in yourself and want to change. Place a smaller picture of how you want to be in a mental sling. Then imagine pulling the sling as far back as possible so that the desirable picture becomes even smaller than it was. Then let go. Imagine the smaller picture of the state you want flying full-force in the direction of the undesirable state and crashing entirely through the picture, replacing the negative image with the positive one. This also works only with repetition and speed. Making sound effects out loud when the slingshot snaps will really help to really intensify the experience.

Remember always that you are in charge of your own brain and you have the power to change pictures in your mind. That's right, you are in control.

Transform Negative Feelings about Yourself through Anchoring

Do you remember the classic story of Pavlov and his dog? Pavlov was a Russian psychologist who demonstrated that when a dog was exposed to food and a particular sound enough times, then the dog would salivate in response to the sound alone. Pavlov gave food to the dog. The dog salivated when exposed to the food. Then Pavlov rang a bell when giving the food to the dog. After a few trials, Pavlov only rang the bell. To his surprise, the dog began salivating as if the food was given. The dog associated the sound of the bell with food.

Humans do the same thing. Consider my friend who repeatedly failed math tests. He associated math tests with a punishing father. Every time my friend saw a math test, he experienced the same emotions as when his father was criticizing him. In other words, the fear of his father became anchored to the experience of taking math tests. In order to perform in math exams, my friend would have to cut the emotional link between a response to his father and the experience of writing a math exam. The technique I will show you now will help you in business or even personal situations where you may find yourself unconsciously responding to negative experiences in your past.

1.) *Identify the negative feeling.* Let's say you are experiencing fear. You may be afraid to make a particular phone call.

2.) *Recreate the negative feeling and anchor it by touching your ear or wrist.* By touching your ear or wrist you are creating an association in your mind so that when you touch the ear, you are creating a stimulus that produces a conditioned negative response. To test the strength of the anchor, "fire it." Touch your ear and examine the feelings that may come up. You want to be sure that the anchor produces the negative response.

3.) *Think of something that always causes you to have a strong positive feeling.* Anchor it by touching a different part of the body (could be your right knee or right hand.) Think of another positive feeling and anchor it again. Repeat this process, stacking five or more positive feelings until you reach the point at which you experience a wave of positive feelings when you touch your right knee or right hand.

4.) *Rid yourself of the negative feelings by replacing them with positive feelings.* This is called anchor collapsing. You do this by triggering both the positive and negative feelings simultaneously. What will happen is your mind will be thrown into a state of confusion and a new, different state will emerge. The pattern will break, making way for a new one.

It is common for us to transition from one emotional state to another and then to another and another in a single day. We are emotional beings. Anchors often work in chains with one link affecting the next one. Sometimes it is useful to create a chain of anchors so that one chain will stimulate the next one, building up to a sequence of states. Consider a theater actor about to go out on stage who paces himself through a sequence of states until he is mentally focused and prepared to go out on stage and perform his best. You can design a chain of anchors in the same sense to help you get into the state you want at times when the shift from the current state to your desired positive state seems to big of a transition for one step.

For instance, let's say that your current state is "furious" but your desired state is "relaxed." This might seem like a huge transition in the singular, overbearing moment of being furious. However, if you just step from "furious" to "agitated," then it might seem a little more possible. Then if you just step from "agitated" to "worried," it might seem even more possible. If you find yourself "worried," step towards "curious." You can choose another step between "curious" and "relaxed," but it might already be visible to you how you can be in a sudden state of relaxation if you were just in a state of worry and ready to take another step. To make these steps, you will have to be using your anchors. Perhaps you can touch your inner wrist or tap your right heel on the floor, touching whichever body part you have chosen to connect with your emotional states.

One of the most useful places to use anchors is in the ever-panicky scenario (to some) of public speaking. For many, public speaking is the most difficult task to carry out and has apparently become the number one fear in the United States. You might find yourself drenched in sweat, losing your voice, shaking, stumbling, or becoming red in front of a group of people who cannot take their eyes off of you and you alone. If you are one of these people and I've struck accord with a particular phobia of yours, perhaps the phobia of all phobias, then learning how to use anchors is for you.

The following is a task you can perform with a friend in order to get your performance anchors in play and use them the next time you are about to give a speech or presentation:

First think of a situation where you are going to speak aloud or perform some task on stage and picture a big line drawn on the ground in front of you. Make sure it's big and bold enough for you to jump over and back.

1.) Standing on one side of the line, identify your most pleasant, favorite, empowering state. Identify what this state is with your partner.

Your partner will then tell you: "Remember a time when you were _____(whatever the state is). See what you saw, feel what you felt, hear what you heard. Really be in the state."

2.) Then jump over the line and be inside of that experience. Make it vivid enough so you feel as if you were there.

Feel what your hands are doing and create an anchor. Perhaps touch your left palm with your right thumb.

3.) Step back to the original side of the line and break state and repeat the exercise with a second experience of your best state, the same emotional state you triggered before.

Your partner will then prepare you for the upcoming public performance or presentation by telling you "Think of a time when you will utilize this state."

4.) Jump back to the other side of the line and trigger your anchor with your right thumb in your left palm and your partner will ask you to see, hear, and feel what the upcoming performance or presentation will be like.

Remember that anchors do not need to be conditioned over long periods of time in order to become established, but repeated practice will reinforce the anchoring. Internal experience is considered to be significant, behaviorally, as the explicit measurable responses. In other words, NLP states that what you internally feel or create in your mind is as much a response than any kind of physical reward or constitution such as the salivation of Pavlov's dog. The more intense the experience that the individual is having at the time the anchor is set, the stronger the response will be when the anchor is triggered or "fired off" later. Phobias are an example of powerful anchors that, in most cases, are established in a single, intense experience. We will discuss how to be rid of phobias in the next section. Note that anchors can be established in all representational systems, as well as their component parts so use all the senses and as many feelings as you can muster as stimuli for setting and then triggering an anchor.

Whether you notice it or not, people in their everyday living are constantly creating and utilizing powerful anchors and most of the time it is a completely unconscious behavior. Keep in mind how powerful language acts as an anchor and that there are single words that can elicit very strong positive or negative responses. An exciting outcome of your training may be to become more in control of the anchoring that you do naturally to produce the responses you really want in yourself and in others.

Reprogramming the Brain

Although all the methods we have discussed thus far have involved a reprogramming of the brain, whether you were reprogramming how you see something, how it feels to you, or how you will react to it, NLP calls one specific method the actual "Reprogramming" of the brain. You can use this to change a specific memory in the past that has caused you pain and eliminate emotional anchor that you have placed inside of it.

For example, think of a time when someone rejected you. Throughout your life, you may occasionally look back and remember that occasion and feel hurt, sad, or angry still. Later in life, if you feel rejected again, your mind will revert back to that first emotional experience and you will react to this new experience as you reacted then, hurt, sad, and angry again. You have deep emotional roots buried in this singular experience.

You will attempt to avoid rejection just to save yourself from experiencing the same pain, but it will never work because you will continue reverting and reverting and holding onto all that pain. I want you to think instead that your mind is a magnificent, priceless VCR. You are about to record over that experience with something worth watching again. You are going to manipulate your memory in order to achieve power.

Step 1:

I want you to go back and experience the last forty seconds of that event—the one that caused you so much emotional distress. I want you to see the person who is saying these things to you. Hear what they are saying. Feel the way you felt when you were actually in that experience. Close your eyes and begin … What feelings did you get as you played the event in your head? (Hurt, sad, angry?)

Step 2:

This time, do the same as Step 1 but with a few changes. I want you to think you are sitting in a movie theater and watching the event unfold on the movie screen. Change the following about the person who is saying the things that made you feel unwell.

1.) Change this person's nose to a big, red clown nose.

2.) Change the person's voice to sound like Mickey Mouse or the Chipmunks.

3.) Picture this person picking his or her nose while talking.

When ready to play the movie, make sure that those three things are happening at the same time with the person who is saying the things that made you feel unwell … Let's play the movie!!

Step 3:

Now Let's play the movie in slow motion. You see the big red clown nose and the person picking their nose. You also hear the Mickey Mouse or Chipmunk voice as the person is saying the things that they said.

Step 4:

I want you to float out of your movie seat and go sit by the projector. I want you to observe yourself sitting in the seat watching yourself on the big screen as incident is playing. Everything is the same as in Step 2. The big red clown nose, the Mickey Mouse or Chipmunk voice, and the picking of his or her nose are all in play while they are speaking. I want you to fast forward through the film.

Step 5:

Now think of this incident of rejection. What feelings are you getting? Your sad, hurt, and angry feelings should be gone. That's how you can reprogram your mind. You have successfully recorded over the tape with a much lighter, positive movie.

You can use this same technique for any phobias that you might have as well. It will prove to be just as effective. After all, a phobia is rooted in a deep memory of yours that you simply will not let go. So whichever one irks you most. You can be cured! Think about a phobia that you think you simply cannot escape. Public speaking. Spiders. Heights. Suffocation. Clowns. Whatever your phobia is, no matter what anybody says about it being senseless, ridiculous, or even curable, you won't have any of it. You cannot see how it is possible to be rid of this intense, unstoppable fear that you may have been holding onto your entire life. Well, open your eyes. This fear you are holding onto is only holding you back. It is the access of point of almost all of your fear and by curing one phobia, you are disarming the sensation it provokes along with all the negative effects it has on you. Be freed. Go back over the steps for "Reprogramming the Brain" and insert an incident you have had in the past involving your phobia. Instead of adding a Mickey Mouse or Chipmunk voice to the equation, add circus or cartoon-like music instead. Note the feelings of liberation (or silliness) when you are done.

Chapter Ten:
Creating Rapport
Instantaneously

"Anything is possible in the presence of good rapport."

—*Milton Erickson*

When you look at the most charismatic leaders, you will notice one of the most fundamental skills they share: the ability to create instantaneous rapport with anyone. Rapport is a deep and unconscious connection with another person, a mutual feeling that you have a lot in common with them. When you are in good rapport with people in your life, whether they are your friends or clients or loved ones, they will trust you as they think you are just like them. Good rapport fosters understanding and it is a skill that can be learned. The ability to create rapport is the foundation of great communication and outstanding leadership.

While you may feel most comfortable spending time with people who seem to be just like you, the real world is packed with an amazing variety of different types of people. All these people have their own special skills and opinions and backgrounds from which you can learn and benefit. Rapport is the key to success and it influences both your personal and professional life. It allows you to appreciate differences and work with them, assisting you in becoming a well-rounded person, knowledgeable in a variety of subjects opposed to just a few. Ultimately, achieving good rapport with people preserves your time, money, and energy because instead of thinking, "What is he or she talking about?" during an entire conversation, you can sympathize, become a part of their world and instead of retaliating, learn.

In order for you to start understanding how you can personally build rapport, ask yourself the following questions:

1.) Consider a person with whom you have rapport. What are the signals that are being sent and received that allow you to distinguish that you are both on the same wavelength? How is your rapport maintained?

2.) In contrast, consider a person with whom you have no rapport, but would like to. What signals are being sent and received that allow you to believe there is no connection between the two of you? What makes your rapport difficult?

3.) What can you learn from your experience with the first person that you can apply to your experience with the second? What can strengthen your chances for creating rapport?

By being more flexible in your behavior or thoughts about the second person, you may find that you can create rapport with them through simple stages. Perhaps you need to take extra time to get to know them better and find out what's important to them, rather than expecting them to adapt to you and your style of communicating. In terms of creating rapport, it is important to understand that *you* are the message being communicated. Your thoughts and your beliefs are being translated through your words, pictures (i.e. body language), and sounds. If you do not appear confident when relaying a message, people will pick that up and not listen any further. They will only believe in you as much as you believe in yourself. Confidence is one of the easiest things to detect in a person. You can see it in someone who isn't even speaking, who might just be standing in a room communicating through other elements.

In 1967, Dr. Albert Mehrabian, a professor at U.C.L.A., did a study on the relative importance of verbal and nonverbal messages when people communicate their feelings and attitudes. According to Dr. Mehrabian, the impact of communication is less dependent upon words than we think. With his research, he found that 55 percent of the effectiveness of any communication is due to the physiology of an individual, 38 percent is a result of the vocal tonality and only 7 percent is a result of actual words[5]. In order to become outstanding communicators, we must have developed all aspects of communication.

Physiology

Physiology simply refers to what we are doing with our bodies. It is the determining factor of how others perceive us upon a first meeting. For example, have you ever met a person you instantly liked? Or a person you didn't trust right away? These first impressions have a huge impact on how people will respond to you in the future. When I discuss physiology, I refer to how you hold yourself. Do you maintain eye contact or do you look down when someone looks at you? Do you walk with purpose or amble to your destination? Do you project confidence or do you appear fearful? Our physiology and

---

5   McConnell, *The Health Care Supervisor*, 136.

gestures started to be used effectively before we even learned how to talk. When a baby has had enough milk, he or she will shake its head from side to side, rejecting the milk. This is why shaking the head from side to side is considered a "no." If 55 percent of what influences people is physiology, then we need to learn how it works.

The power of physiology is so strong, it even has the ability to affect and create your emotional states. A friend of mine who is a mental health practitioner told me a story. He once held a seminar on how to alleviate depression. Most of the participants in his study suffered from long-term, chronic depression. At the beginning of the seminar, my friend asked the participants to act as if they were the happiest people on earth. He asked them to laugh, move with a brisk pace, throw their shoulders back, breathe deeply from their chests and maintain an erect body posture. After two hours, he asked them about their level of depression. Most participants stated that they had forgotten about their depression and some even stated that they felt cured. By changing their physiology, they had changed their emotional states. Their brains were getting messages from their physiology to be alert and vital and resourceful. It is virtually impossible to remain depressed when one's physiology demonstrates a positive state of mind.

Whenever you feel that you simply cannot do something, the best way to get yourself to try is to simply act like you can do it. Most likely you will fool your mind and be able to complete any task. Stand the way you would stand if you knew how to do it. Breathe the way you would be breathing if you were successfully completing the task. As soon as you are standing and breathing the way you would as if you could do whatever it was you said you couldn't do, you will feel that it is truly possible. It's a remarkable gift from our physiology. Whenever you feel you cannot approach that man or woman in the bar, whenever you feel that you can't speak to your employer about a pay raise, change your state to an empowering one and act as if the task has already been completed and you have been fulfilled because of it. You are already smiling, already breathing with confidence and delight, already gratified before it has been done.

This works the same way with exercise. If you are sitting on an exercise bike, forty-five minutes in but pushing for an hour, you might already be tired and short of breath. You might be telling yourself that this workout is hard, that you're tired and you still have quite some time to go. Your physiology will start to match your thoughts and you'll begin to pant and sweat profusely and slump over the digital read-out. If you simply sit up straight and begin to direct your breathing to a normal rate, you will find yourself recovered in a matter of moments.

Ninety-three percent of our communication is managed by the unconscious. Some of the physiological factors that fall under this category are hand placing and gestures. There have been some interesting findings about what some of the most common gestures really communicate. For instance, when a child lies, he or she will typically put their hands behind their back. When men do not want to converse, they often shove their hands in their pockets. Pointing is one of the most annoying gestures anyone can use while speaking and many times we won't even realize we are doing it while everyone around us slowly becomes uncomfortable as a result. In some countries, such as Malaysia and the Philippines, finger pointing at a person is an insult and a gesture reserved only for pointing at animals.

Many of our unconscious physiological gestures are signs of approval or rejection. The following charts are entertaining interpretations of many of these gestures.

Approval

Playing With the Hair	Indicates highest satisfaction towards the person speaking but carries connotations of affection
Kissing	By slightly puckering lips into a kiss, person expresses approval towards topic being discussed or person with whom they are speaking
Lip Licking	Conveys approval towards topic or person speaking
Lip Biting	This portrays great emotional involvement and is an invitation for further discussion
Leaning Forward	Indicates interest in topic and person speaking
Opening Arms and Legs	Invitation for further discussion
Putting Finger or Object in Mouth	Sexual connotations towards person speaking or topic being discussed
Casually Touching	Signifies empathy

Pressing Tongue Against Inside of Cheek	Beginning to approve of a subject but still considering
Moving Objects Toward Oneself	Represents an attempt to take the lead in a discussion

Rejection

Leaning the Body Backwards	Indicates a withdrawal from a topic
Throat Clearing	Conveys a rejection of an argument
Rubbing Nose with a Finger	Expresses rejection of a topic
Moving Objects Away From Oneself	Represents withdrawal from conversation
Brushing Away Dust or Crumbs from Table	Signifies closing of a discussion

Oftentimes, people will massage or scratch parts of his or her body as a reaction to stress since vein dilation has started to occur. This means that a person's stress has reached its tolerance level so that they have become physically affected. For instance, a person might scratch their head when a topic has created enough stress to result in an actual headache. By massaging one's forehead, a speaker is being signaled to go into more detail since what he is saying is not being understood. By biting the upper lip, a person is stating that they are lacking sexual fulfillment so it is usually signaled towards a person to whom they are attracted. This works the same way when a woman plays with her necklace or a man plays with his necktie. On the other hand, biting the lower lip shows a lack of affection (the complete opposite!) Scratching or rubbing the ear signifies that the person is displaying repressed sexual impulses about the topic or person with whom they are speaking. When a person lifts their left toe but keeps their heel on the ground, it can be assumed that they prefer that another person speak. In contrast, when they lift their right toe, keeping their heel on the ground, they are signifying that they wish to speak. By pointing the right foot towards someone, take a note of what is actually being pointed at. Whatever it is, the person pointing takes a particular interest towards it. If we are talking to a person and notice that they are pointing their foot towards somebody else, it means that they would unconsciously wish to be talking to this other person. Obviously, if they are pointing their foot towards an exit room, we know that they want out!

Stated previously, the first meeting with a person will strongly impact the way he or she will view you thereafter. One of the most noticeable physiological components—especially important in the business world—is the all-telling handshake. Of course in places like Japan where handshaking is not customary, this may be entirely irrelevant. However, for the rest of us, handshakes can provide a sea of information. In 2001, William Chaplin at the University of Alabama conducted a study of handshakes (Bryant, 2001, 1). He found that confident people use firm handshakes while shy people do not. He also found that women who are open to new ideas use firm handshakes. Men use the same handshakes whether they are open to new ideas or not. There are three types of handshakes:

a. Dominant handshake: is when you shake your hands and your palm is face down.

b. Submissive handshake: is the opposite of the dominant handshake and entails offering your hand with the palm face up. This symbolically gives the other person the upper hand.

c. Equality handshake: is when two dominant people shake hands and an unconscious power struggle takes place as each person attempts to turn the other's palm into the submissive position. This creates a feeling of equality and mutual respect because neither is prepared to give in to the other.

The majority of top executives use the dominant handshake. What does your handshake say about you?

If you want to become more skilled in rapport building, decide what kind of physiology you want to demonstrate. Also, watch the other person's physiology. If you want to be in rapport with them, match what they are doing with their body. The process for creating a deep, unconscious rapport is to match and mirror the person with whom you are communicating. If you match and mirror body posture, head tilt, and gestures and combine them with similar volume and tempo of speech (which we will discuss next), you will find yourself in rapport with another person. The secret to making the rapport techniques work is that you must match and mirror in a way that the other person you are communicating with is not consciously aware of it. This means if you are matching and mirroring gestures the person uses, wait until it's your turn to speak and make similar gestures, being careful not to fall into mimicry. You could choose four ways of matching a person's physiology. You can match their whole body, adjusting to their postural shifts, gestures, and movements. You can match a few body parts, such as paying close attention to their hand placement and focusing in on only that. You can choose to match only half of their body, taking note of how they hold their upper body or their lower body. Do they cross their arms more or do they cross their legs? Or you can simply match their head and shoulders; do they nod their head frequently? Are they constantly shrugging their shoulders? How about their face? What sort of statements result in the wrinkling of their nose or rising of their eyebrows? If the mentioning of political figures makes your co-worker widen her eyes and reply shortly and closed off, then you know your conversation will not flourish. The eyes are also a part of physiology that tell you a lot about what a person is thinking or trying to say, or which representational system they are referring to. Since eyes are so prominent a discussion, there is an entire chapter devoted to them following this one.

Keep in mind that you can mirror the physiology of someone great in order to develop your own greatness by legitimate studying. Think about five people who have powerful physiologies that you would like to mirror. How do these physiologies differ from yours? How do these people sit, stand, or move? What are some of their most prominent facial expressions or hand gestures? Take a moment to stand like one of these people and make a facial expression you've seen them make before. How do you feel? It is often possible to achieve an exact experience of someone who you genuinely admire simply by mirroring his or her physiology. If you can get a tape from someone like Martin Luther King Jr., you can test out this technique for yourself. Stand how he stands, breathes how he breathes, talk like he talks and note what you feel.

People take drugs, overheat, smoke cigarettes and drink alcohol simply to change their mental states via their physiological system. NLP allows you to change your state naturally but just as dramatically as those external sources would.

Tonality

Tonality is one of these factors that, on the surface, seems not to have much impact. Most people believe that what we say is more important than how we say it. This is untrue. People respond mainly to the "how." To demonstrate the power of tonality, I invite you to complete a small exercise. Read the following sentences aloud, putting emphasis on the italicized word.

"*I* never said he lied"

"I *never* said he lied"

"I never *said* he lied"

"I never said *he* lied"

"I never said he *lied*"

This is exactly the same sentence with the same words in the same order, yet the shift in emphasis dramatically changes the meaning. People respond subconsciously to the style of our communication, often disregarding the words. Intonations are patterns, or melodies in the pitch of your voice. Using intonations in a sentence will elicit a certain state from the person with whom you are speaking. If you ask them a question, you will sound your voice with a higher pitch towards the end of your sentence as in, "Will you *call me*?" When making a statement, keep the tone of your voice straight and flat as in, "These are the two items I want." When you are executing a command, the tone of your voice should be lower and decreasing on the command such as, "Once you simply *sign this offer*, you will be happy and excited."

In matching a person's intonation when building rapport, be sure to adopt the tone and breathing pattern of the other person. If they are using a low tone and speaking in a soft voice at a slow speed, alter your tone so that it is also low, be sure to speak softly and breathe similarly. This will ensure that all your thoughts and ideas are on the same wavelength and conversation will flow easiest.

You can also match a person indirectly by what is called "cross-over mirroring." Using cross-over mirroring helps to keep you from mimicking the other person. You can use one aspect of your behavior to match a different aspect of the other person's behavior; for example you can adjust the tempo of your voice to match the other person's rate of breathing or you can pace the other person's eye blinks with your head nods.

Words

The English language contains 615,000 words, not including technical and scientific terms. Of those thousands of words, everyone has a slightly different meaning for each one. In addition, people often structure their sentences, sometimes deleting portions, which often leads to confusion on the part of the other person. For example, John might say, "I am very excited." The other person does not know what John is excited about and can only assume what the source of excitement is. Alex might say, "I am not sure I want to do it." Many meanings can be ascribed to this sentence. From the content of the statement, one does not know what Alex is not sure about, what he is not sure about doing, or how sure he really is about being unsure. I am certain that you have had an experience when you said something and the other person interpreted it completely different from what you intended. Learn how to ask the right questions to elicit the true meaning behind the statements you are receiving. By doing so, you will eliminate most misunderstandings.

A person's representational system can also be decoded through the words he or she is using. Representational system predicates are the process words (verbs, adverbs, adjectives) which people use in their communication to represent their experience internally, whether by visual, auditory, or kinesthetic means. Below is a list of words people might say that will reveal what representational system they are using so that you can forfeit yours and adopt theirs in order to maintain good rapport. These might be especially useful in the business world.

VISUAL (see)	angle, appear, aspect, conspicuous, demonstrate, dream, example, focus, foresee, glance, hindsight, horizon, idea, illusion, illustrate, image, inspect, look, notice, obscure, observe, obvious, outlook, perception, picture, pinpoint, scene, scope, scrutinize, see, show, sight, sketchy, survey, vague, view, vision, watch, witness
AUDITORY (say/hear)	announce, articulate, communicate, converse, discuss, divulge, earshot, enunciate, gossip, hear, hush, inquire, interview, listen, loud, mention, noise, oral, proclaim, pronounce, remark, report, ring, rumor, say, silence, sound, speak, speechless, squeal, state, talk, tell, tone, utter, vocal voice

KINESTHETIC (feel/do)	active, affected, bearable, callous, charge, concrete, emotional, feel, firm, flow, foundation, grasp, grip, hanging, hassle, heated, hold, hunch, hustle, intuition, motion, muddled, pressure, rush, sensitive, shallow, shift, softly, solid, sore, stir, stress, structured, support, tension, tied, touch, unbearable, unsettled

The following is a list of phrases that might be used to point his or her preferred representational system:

VISUAL (see)	an eyeful, bird's eye view, dim view, get a perspective on, in view of, mental image, naked eye, plainly see, short-sighted, staring off into space, under your nose, appears to me, catch a glimpse of, eye to eye, in light of, looks like, paint a picture, showing off, take a peek, up front, beyond a shadow of a doubt, clear-cut, in person, make a scene, mind's eye, see to it, sight for sore eyes, tunnel vision

AUDITORY (say/hear)	after-thought, clearly expressed, earful, hold your tongue, keynote speaker, pay attention to, outspoken, state your purpose, tongue-tied, utterly, within hearing range, blabber mouth, call on, express yourself, loud and clear, tattle-tale, word for word, describe in detail, give an account of, inquire into, rings a bell, to tell the truth, unheard of
KINESTHETIC (feel/do)	come to grips with, firm foundation, get a load of this, heated argument, hot-head, lay card on table, not following you, slipped my mind, start from scratch, too much a hassle, boils down to, control yourself, floating on thin air, get in touch with, hand-in hand, light-headed, pull some strings, smooth operator, stiff upper lip, cool/calm/collected, get a handle on, hang in there! hold on! sharp as a tack, so-so, underhanded

If you can take note of what kind of representational systems the person with whom you are speaking prefers, then you will be able to develop better rapport with them by speaking always in whichever one they prefer. It will be easier for this person to understand what you are saying and process it faster. The following is an example of a conversation in which both people are speaking in terms of their own representational systems and getting nowhere.

Debbie: I don't see how you are saving me money.

Brian: Listen to me. Hear how I am saving you money. I am discounting you 15 percent.

Debbie: I still don't see how you are saving me money.

Only until one of them adopts the representational system of the other does the other understand.

Brian: Let me show you on this paper how I will give you a 15 percent discount.

Debbie: Great! Now I understand!

That is how fast rapport can be created. The only way you can make this happen is by removing pride from your conversation. This is a difficult task because most people are so stubborn in their pride, that they'd rather be misunderstood than compromise their language or point of view for another. Pride is merely a perception we create to feel better about ourselves. So if pride is a perception, then it really doesn't exist. How many fights in the past would have been over quickly if you had simply said you were sorry? I'm sure plenty of them. Is your pride worth you not making money or keeping your relationship? I hope not. Get rid of it.

Pacing and Leading

Once you master the detection of someone's representational system and are able to communicate effectively in it, you will want to take the position of leader in the conversation by mastering another technique: pacing and leading. Building great relationships requires that you pace other people. In NLP, you can think of pacing like running alongside a moving vehicle. If you tried to jump onto a moving vehicle, you would probably fall off. The only successful way to jump onto a moving vehicle is to gather enough speed, run alongside the vehicle until you are both at the same speed and then make your way on. This is the same with people. The purpose of building rapport with people, and the purpose we are discussing it in this book is because in building rapport, you are able to lead any conversation and convince anyone to adhere to your point of view simply by the way you are communicating with them. Rapport builds trust and when you are being trusted, you can say just about anything with validity and the power of influence. The most successful way to accomplish this is by genuinely listening to the other person, acknowledging them, and being patient with trying to understand where they are coming from. You must be willing to pace consistently before you take the lead in a conversation. By pacing you will be able to pick up this person's belief systems as presented to you with their physiology, tone, and word choice, matching them to ease conversation, and using their communicative tendencies to your fullest benefit. It's like fighting fire with fire. You're using their language to get what you want.

If you can get yourself to any worthy car dealership, you might be able to catch an effective salesperson in action and recognize successful pacing and leading. Effective salespeople will listen faithfully to what their customers' needs are and what they truly want before they ever try to sell them a single thing. Customers resent being had or being easily sold but when they are approached by a salesperson that seems to really care about their needs, the possibility of purchasing becomes less intimidating and more likely.

The Meta Model

NLP gives us a method called the Meta Model that enables us to uncover the real meaning behind what people are saying despite their often limiting selection of words. This can be used at any one of those opportune times you just wanted to say, "Spit it out!" but wisely held your tongue. Simply think of yourself as an excavator. The archaeological findings for which you are strenuously digging are the actual meanings behind what people are saying or not saying. Instead of guessing, instead of wondering, instead of prying, wouldn't it be nice to just "get it" without all the hard work? "Getting" what people mean does not have to be strenuous. This model will help you resurrect the real pictures people are considering in their minds despite the little words they use to describe them, also known as their perception filters. You will be able to excavate the real heart of the matter, whatever it may be, by precise usage of the Meta Model.

We mentioned earlier that our brains work constantly at filtering out unneeded information to avoid a system overload. Deletion refers to a process whereby humans subconsciously pay attention to certain aspects of their experience and ignore other sensory information. Without deletion our brains would certainly crash with too much information. However, we may delete important information in the process, especially when we are trying to communicate our thoughts to other people. Distortion refers to a process whereby we misrepresent our experiences. We distort observations and experiences. We remember experiences in an altered form and interpret them incorrectly. Generalization simply means vagueness. We don't describe a situation or idea in enough detail so that all people might understand and grasp full meaning.

The Meta Model offers a series of questions that enable you to overcome the deletions, distortions, and generalizations that people make. The questions will probably be recognizable to you since you might ask some of them of yourself when you are trying to clarify meaning. To have them down on paper will simply help you to become more conscious of them so that you can use them systematically in trying to understand other people. In other words, you will be using questions that you usually ask yourself internally to question people you are communicating with externally with elegance and in good rapport.

The following three charts will help you recognize patterns of deletions, distortions, and generalizations you would typically hear someone use and questions you can ask to help them be more specific.

Meta Model Pattern Deletion

NLP Meta Model Pattern	What you hear	What you ask
Unspecified verbs	They irritated me	How specifically did they irritate you?
Judgments	You are mean	Where did you get this information and what are your facts?
Comparisons	He's smarter than me	Smarter than you in what?

Meta Model Pattern Distortion

NLP Meta Model Pattern	What you hear	What you ask
Complex equality	With a house like that, they must be rich	How does having a house like that make them rich?
Cause and effect	I made him feel really bad	How exactly did you do that?
Mind reading	You're going to be angry	How do you know for sure?

Meta Model Pattern Generalization

NLP Meta Model Pattern	What you hear	What you ask
Possibility statements	I couldn't … it's not possible	Who says so? Why?
Necessity statements	We should do this …	What would happen if we didn't?
Universal statements	We *always* go this way	What would happen if we went another way?

Sometimes, when people want something badly enough, they will believe something to be true even when there may be evidence to disprove them. For instance, you might go to an event like a Spelling Bee for your child and come across a parent who simply will not believe that their child has misspelled anything. There are the judges' testimonies along with the testimonies of everyone else in the audience, and perhaps even an audio recording to be used in cases such as these. Still the parent will listen to no reason. They will delete the wrong spelling, distort the whole Spelling Bee itself, and generalize that all Spelling Bees are pre-fixed and unfair. Using the Meta Model would help to eliminate this ruckus and to a certain extent, bring overall truth to the table. Someone just has to step in and use it.

The Meta Model enables you to use language to gain clarity and truly become a part of someone's experience. All it consists of is asking questions. It will help not only you as a listener but the person you are asking so that they might re-evaluate their patterns of thinking and determine new results. Use it when you need to gather more information, or spot your own or other people's limitations, to break habits for yourself and others, and to open up more options and explore new routes. Remember though that in order to effectively use the Meta

Model, you will want to have achieved rapport first or else you will sound like an interrogator. Make sure you are clear about what your outcome is, you don't want to persist with a "what if" cycle of questioning because it will not only irritate the person being questioned but it will also provide you with a bulk of unneeded information. Use a soft tone of voice and gentle speaking tempo. Be focused without rushing and take your time without wasting time. Use soft beginning for your questions such as, "I wonder if …" or "Can you tell me …" or even "I'm curious …" From time to time, repeat back the other person's words, you must use their exact words in order for them to feel you were truly listening. Try the Meta Model on yourself first to see what works best. After all, we constantly question ourselves anyway, but let's try questioning ourselves to achieve better beliefs and remove negative limits. Ask yourself what you're really getting at and you might be surprised at what you find.

The Milton Model

When first studying NLP, it's easy to confuse the Meta Model with the Milton Model because of the alliteration. But do not be distracted by all the M's! The two models are very separate things. The Meta Model is about getting people to be more specific, whereas the Milton Model adopts vague language so that it can be interpreted widely. The Meta Model strives to gather more information, while the Milton Model strives to rise above the detail.

You can look at the Milton Model as a model for hypnosis. It was constructed with the work of Milton H. Erickson in mind, one of the most influential hypnotherapists of our time. Erickson was able to induce trance in his patients and change their thinking patterns so that they felt "healed" of mental ailments or fears. His method consisted of pacing people's reality and putting them into a trance so that he was able to sympathize with what they must be feeling and then gradually led them into healthier, new thinking. By using the specialized language the Milton Model provides for us, you will be also be able to put people under a hypnotic trance as well and help them understand things about themselves and thus communicate with you better. It's important to recognize that a person's behavior doesn't necessarily mean that he or she is a certain way because of what they do. Use solid judgment instead of jumping to conclusions about people. Separating behavior from the person can be key. People can behave in a way that may seem "wrong" or "bad" to you, but perhaps they only behave this way because they lack the inner resources and ability to behave otherwise. Perhaps they feel limited by their environment or any of the negative belief systems we mentioned earlier, or any other belief systems you have not yet considered. Using the Milton Model to relax others and help them look inwardly is a way you can contribute to developing capabilities in themselves or skills in which they can move themselves to a more beneficial environment that would catapult them to unnoticed levels of excellence. In other words, be a gift in their lives and let this be the method!

Keep in mind the purpose of putting people under a trance is not to make them bark like a dog or hand their wallets over to you as entertaining as that might sound to you. Use the hypnotic state to help people access unconscious resources, make changes, and solve their own problems so you don't have to. All you're doing is bringing light to their minds in areas that may have been darkened. All in all, the Milton model is just another connection tool but on a more profound level.

The Milton Model uses all the same patterns as the Meta Model but in a reversed state. So instead of making language more specific, you'll make language more general. Instead of bringing an experience to conscious awareness, you'll aim to access unconscious resources. In business rapport, the Meta Model will help to keep your client externally focused, whereas under the trance of the Milton Model, they will be internally engaged. In its efforts, the Milton Model is effective in bringing the person you are speaking to into utter relaxation.

The way it functions is that when a person makes a deletion, distortion, or generalization, you will use vague language to challenge these filters and take a person into a receptive state so you can help change their line of thinking. If someone makes a deletion by using unspecified verbs such as: "He irritated me," you can challenge the statement by saying something like: "As you make sense of this in your own time ..." If they make a judgment like: "They are mean an inconsiderate," you can respond with, "Remember that you have been through some tough times and survived them well." If they make a generalization about possibility such as, "I couldn't ... it's not possible," you can say to them, "You can become more successful ... you are capable of discovering new ways." By making distortions such as "I made him feel really bad," a person might be ready to crumble into a nest of guilt, but you can prevent this entire experience by saying to them, "Just breathe. With each breath, you can relax more and more ..." and stray them away from the negative feelings of guilt.

With the Milton Model you can use tag questions to invite agreement, even if the person is initially feeling doubtful. This will speed up their processing of the information and give them an easy option to simply agree with your positive suggestions. Tag questions are added to the end of statements and they look like "This is easy isn't it?" and "You can, can't you?" The effect is that the statement in front of the tag question goes directly to the unconscious mind and is acted upon.

Once you have successfully put a person into a trance, you can start to *embed commands* in their now receptive mind. The purpose of an embedded command is to send directions straight into the unconscious mind with the conscious mind being unable to detect it. By changing your tone of voice, you can set the command away from the rest of the vague, relaxation language so that the person will not catch it right away. You will want to put your commands into a larger sentence so that the person will not notice the actual commands. In the sentences below, the italicized words are the commands and will be said in more rapid, deeper tone of voice, separate from the soft, gentle tone you would use for the rest of the words.

"You can begin to *relax*."

"I don't know how soon you'll *feel better*."

The above messages are likely to have a much more graceful impact than if you were to give the directions alone: "Relax," "Feel better."

In the same way that you would embed a command, you can also embed a question within a larger sentence structure so it ultimately goes unnoticed. You could say:

"I'm curious to know why you wouldn't accept the offer."

Typically people will respond to the embedded question "Why wouldn't you accept the offer?" without realizing that the question was not asked directly. The listener doesn't refuse to answer the question because it is embedded within a statement about the speaker's curiosity.

You can also give a command in its negative form by stating what you do want to occur but preceding this statement with the word, "don't." Simply by the way our brains work, we will think of something and respond to it, even if we are told not to. For instance if someone says, "Don't think of a pink elephant," obviously a pink elephant is the first thing that will pop into our minds. We have to think of one just to understand the sentence. To use negative commands effectively you can say the following:

"I don't want you to learn the patterns too fast," obviously implying that you *do* want them to learn the patterns fast.

Making presuppositions are also great ways of getting a person to do what you want. The way they are stated makes presuppositions especially powerful: you give the other person a series of choices, but all choices presuppose the response you want. A track coach might tell a hesitant runner, "Do you want to relax prior to running 2 miles?" This will presuppose that the runner will run the two miles though the runner feels like he has an option for relaxation in the matter. If you were a massaged therapist, you could tell your client, "You may be curious what part of your body you want massaged first." This presupposes that both sides of the body will be massaged; the only question is which will be first. You can make use of the word "or" but presupposing that at least one of several alternatives will take place, making the other person feel that they have many options, a desirable scenario. You might say, "I don't know if your dry cleaning or your car will be taken care of first."

Using vague language is powerful when it helps you get other people into a desirable state in which you can make suggestions and most likely have them be accepted. It will help you connect with larger groups of people and get into rapport with people you don't know very well. When you are vague, it leaves room for people to come to their own conclusions and make their own decisions without even recognizing the dramatic nudge you may have given them. This will make their decisions more powerful and long lasting for them. The Milton Model can also help your internal dialogue by arousing your natural curiosity and assisting you in finding times in your past when you were at your best, and taking you back to those resourceful states.

Throughout your day, you often move through series of experiences, which become trance-like once you catch yourself drifting off or daydreaming. This is not always a bad thing! Daydreaming and being in trance-like situations can be relaxing and inviting for meditative practice. You are more likely to relax and rest, almost like taking a mini-nap but while awake. You are also more likely to be open to new ideas and wandering within your mind is simple exercise for new goal setting. You might become more creative and inspired while daydreaming and take these ideas with you when you "wake up" and are able to work with them more actively. The only downside to daydreaming is of course when you do not act on creative impulses or when you replay in your mind various anxieties that tend to worry you.

You can use rapport to connect with people, learn from them, influence them, and the more you practice the closer you will come to mastering communication with anyone, anywhere. Just remember as important as it is to build rapport, it is just as important to be able to break rapport. Why? You may want to break rapport at opportune times when you are closing a deal or you've gotten enough information for the moment and cannot absorb much more. Perhaps you're in rapport with someone but you notice someone else in the room from whom you might benefit more. Sometimes you're just too tired for any more talk, or you're too busy to carry on any further. Maybe you feel a conflict about to arise as in the topics of sex, politics or religion. The easiest way to break rapport is to simply mismatch the other person. Mismatching is the opposite of matching and mirroring. If you are in conversation but wish to immediately stop, try these three techniques:

1.) Change your physiology. You may want to physically create some space, break your eye contact or raise your eyebrows. These are subtle ways to kindly end conversation. If you want to be more forceful, turn your back to them.

2.) Change your sound. Alter your voice intonation or volume. Speak louder or softer, higher or lower or even resort to silence.

3.) Change your word choice. This is when you need most to practice the word so many of us are often afraid to use: "No." You can lighten this word with a: "No, thank you," but even that one seems hard to use at times.

Remember always to be considerate when breaking rapport as in the cases of dealing with loved ones or close friends. Give positive, concise feedback that communicates that you care for them as a person and would love to listen to their story but at the proper place and time. You don't want to use mismatching simply to be uncompassionate.

CHAPTER ELEVEN:
TO SEE OR NOT TO SEE

"The real voyage of discovery consists not in seeking new landscapes, but in having new eyes."

—*Marcel Proust*

It has long been said that the eyes are windows to the soul. Although our eyes are a mere component of our physiology, it is by far the most all-telling. By using your eyes, you are able to follow not only the shoulder shrugs or head tilts or finger pointing of your neighbors but to also tap into the deepest fundamentals behind their language simply by following their eyes. When you have successfully created rapport with someone, pay close attention to his or her eye movements and patterns so that you may determine what representational system he or she is using.

First it would be beneficial to consider where the information our eyes process is actually being sent before we start asking how. As the central processing unit for all our emotions, memories, external stimuli and internal response, the brain is a complex organ to say the least. To understand how an individual processes internal information and to predict how he or she will act upon it, we need to first understand how the brain is organized.

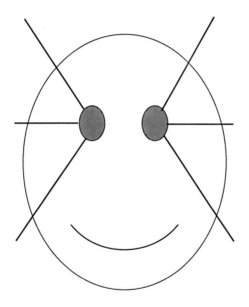

6

The cortex of each hemisphere is divided into four areas called lobes. The frontal lobe is primarily involved in planning,

---

6   http://www.brainviews.com/abfiles/DrxMedlobes.jpg

demonstrating, decision-making, and purposeful behavior. The parietal lobe represents the body in the brain. It receives sensory information from the body. Part of the occipital lobe is devoted to vision and is often called the visual cortex. The temporal lobe appears to have several important functions, including hearing, perception, and memory.

One effective way of figuring out what representation system you prefer and to best distinguish what representation systems other people are using, answer the following question: What was the color of the house you lived in as a child? Take a moment and remember ... To answer that question, 90 percent of you looked up and to the left. For right-handed people, and even some left-handed, visually remembered images are accessed in this way. It is stored on the upper left side of the brain. How would Minnie Mouse look in pants? Take a moment to picture this. This time your eyes probably went up and to the right. That's the place people's eyes go to access constructed images, not memories. Just by looking at a person's eyes, you will be able to tell what sensory system they are accessing and understand their strategies.

Carry on a conversation with a person and observe their eye movements. Ask them questions about memories and notice where their eyes go as they remember. This is an effective way to discern someone's honesty with you. If their eyes are constantly moving up and to the right then they might just be lying to you. You can become an immediate psychic and you haven't even purchased a crystal ball!

Some entertaining questions are entered below to help you track someone's eye movement in conversation:

TO GET	ASK
Visually Remembered Pictures	Which is the darkest room in your house? What was the color of your high school girlfriend or boyfriend's hair? What is the first thing you see every morning? How many windows do you have in your house? What color are the countertops in your kitchen? What colors do you have the most of in your wardrobe?
Visually Constructed Pictures	What would your vehicle look like if it had wings and was made of gold? Imagine yourself with a long tail and purple hair. What would your pet look like if it were 50 times its size?

Auditory Remembered	What was the last thing someone said to you today? What was one of your favorite songs in high school? What's more annoying: the screeching of nails down a chalkboard or someone who can't stop clearing his throat? What's the fifth word in the Star Spangled Banner? Listen in your mind to the trickling of a creek. Who of your acquaintances has the most pleasant voice?
Auditory Constructed	What would you say if someone asked you how we could eliminate hunger in the world? If you could ask any question of our president what would it be? Imagine the sound of a dog bark slowly becoming that of a basketball bounce.
Auditory Internal Dialogue	Internally repeat this question to yourself: What do I care most about in this world?

Kinesthetic Words	Imagine the feeling of ice melting in your hand. What does it feel like to floss? Which is the softest feeling garment that you own? Imagine yourself settling down into a nice hot bath.

The following is an eye-accessing chart that can be used in conversation. It has the image of a human face in the middle and is surrounded by the areas in which a person would point their eyes when accessing information.

Visual Constructed:
Seeing images of things never seen before, or seeing things differently than they were seen before. Example: "What would you look like with purple hair?"

Visual Remembered:
Seeing images of things seen before, in the same way they were seen before. Example: "What does your car look like?"

Auditory Constructed:
Hearing sounds not heard before. Example: "What would a cat sound like if it barked?"

Auditory Remembered:
Remembering sounds heard before. Example: "What was the last song you heard on the radio?"

Kinesthetic:
Feeling emotions, tactile sensations (sense of touch) or feelings of muscle movement. Example: "What does it feel like to crunch ice between your teeth?"

Auditory Digital:
Talking to oneself. Example: "Recite the lyrics of your favorite song to yourself."

Now you can consider that if a person's eyes are moving up and to the left, he is most likely picturing something from his memory. If they look toward the left ear, he listened to something. When the eyes go down and to the right, he may be accessing the kinesthetic part of his representational system. In the same way, if you are having difficulty remembering something, it may be helpful to avert your eyes so that they are pointing to the most accessible area.

CHAPTER TWELVE: ADAPTATION

"Reasonable people adapt themselves to the world. Unreasonable people attempt to adapt the world to themselves. All progress, therefore, depends on unreasonable people."

—*George Bernard Shaw*

Imagine yourself at a dinner party, drink of choice in hand, surrounded by five acquaintances. You've just heard a new joke from a close friend and decide to share it with those around you. Two of them laugh. One of them wrinkles his eyebrows because he doesn't get it. The other one scowls and rolls her eyes at you. She has been offended. Do you ever wonder why people react so differently to identical messages? What makes one person an optimist and the other a pessimist? What makes one person happy on rainy days and another dreadful on a warm, sunny day? Our preferences, yes. But what makes up our preferences?

In creating rapport with someone and maintaining it as well, it's crucial to understand what key the person to whom you are speaking prefers. The key a person prefers depends on their personality. "Personality" is just another word for metaprogram. You can give the most inspiring, driven, motivational message to a person but it will be quickly disregarded if it doesn't connect with him or her on an intellectual and emotional level. If you want to be a master persuader, a master negotiator, a master communicator in general, you will have to know which key works for each person. You have to understand metaprograms.

We already know people will process their information through representational systems and that we can tweak our words and physiologies in order to illustrate effectively what we are trying to say. We know that must filter our experiences to avoid a bombardment of the senses, or system crash, by deleting, distorting, and generalizing. In order to communicate effectively with another person, you have to understand his filters as well. What is he distorting? Deleting? Generalizing? Why?

Metaprograms will help you understand the patterns of behavior people adopt and patterns in which they organize their experience which result in those behaviors. Being able to understand a person's mental patterns and communicating through them is the only way you will ever be able to effectively get your message across and be understood. What's the point of talking to someone if you sound like the Charlie Brown schoolteacher? No point at all. All situations vary but there are five basic metaprogram structures that we will discuss in this chapter. They are the proactive/reactive, the options/procedure, the toward/away from, the internal/external, and the global/detail metaprograms.

Proactive/Reactive

If you are a *proactive* person, it means that you take the initiative to actively get things done. If you see a project that entails a list of procedures and strategies, you take role as the leader and assemble the actions needed to complete the task. And then you work, work, work. Proactive people often have jobs in sales or are typically self-employed. Many times other people, especially those who are reactive, see you as intimidating and too forceful.

As a *reactive* person, you might be rather accepting and wait often for others to begin a task before you decide to respond to it. You might be very analytical, so analytical in fact that you run the risk of doing nothing.

It's quite easy to detect a proactive or reactive personality by the body language being used. A proactive person might have quicker movements, and hold an erect body posture, always ready for a new task. A reactive person will move slower and keep their head down, waiting for someone to make a decision for them. A proactive person will often use phrases such as "Run with it" or "Go for it," while a reactive person might say "Take your time," or "Look before you leap."

Toward/Away from

Either you are going toward something (love, freedom, health, happiness, wealth) or you are going away from something (guilt, sadness, loneliness, anger, poverty). People can find motivation either way. Some people will tell themselves, "I don't want to be in a position where I don't have enough money to have food on the table." This is a statement of "away," as they are trying to stay away from a situation of poverty. Another person would say, "I want to eat fresh so I can live a long life." This is a *toward* value. They are directing their behavior toward health.

Some people use pain to motivate themselves, while other use pleasure. It's all a matter of preference.

People with *away from* patterns will sometimes appear as pessimists to people with *toward* patterns. The *away from* people will have a tendency of noticing what could go wrong and they are most useful in careers involving mechanics and maintenance. It is easy to motivate *away from* people with threats of financial impediments or job loss. People who prefer *toward* patterns might seem like cheery optimists, organizing their actions in the direction of what they would like to move toward such as rewards, benefits, and overall gains.

In rapport, you can easily use the toward/away from pattern to sell whatever you've got if you know in which direction to sell it. You can promote your product, idea, or suggestion by either listing what it does or what it doesn't do, depending on who you're talking to. If you were selling a car, you would either say it was fast and sleek, and luxurious, and hip, or you would say it would not use much gas, and wouldn't cost too much to maintain. You could use the same technique with your husband or wife for example if you wanted to go a tropical vacation during the winter but he or she seemed hesitant. If he or she preferred a *toward* system, you'd mention how warm you would be in the tropics at winter and that you would be finding a romantic, secluded paradise. If he or she was an *away from* person, you would be sure to remark on the fact that tropical places in the winter would keep you away from the tourists and the harshness of your cold winter at home.

To determine whether a person has a *toward* or *away from* value system, ask them questions about what is important to them and then note in which direction their answers take them. You can say: Tell me about one of your favorite life experiences and why it was important to you. Describe one of the environments in which you are happiest. How did you motivate yourself to get up this morning? What was the last thing you said to yourself before getting out of bed?

Options/Procedures

If you are a person who prefers options, this means that you enjoy trying new ways and doing new things. You are always looking for a new edge, an uncharted path, and something wholly unique. You are attracted to variety of things and will often start projects, but get bored with them halfway and pick something else. You will often set rules and procedures but rarely follow them. Phrases such as "possibilities" or "play it by ear" might reveal an *options* person.

A person who prefers procedures, on the other hand, will be happy to follow a set of methodologies and tested techniques. You will often list the series of steps that got you a job or resulted in your chosen pair of running shoes. A *procedures* person might us expressions such as "step by step" or "firstly, secondly."

You can find out which of these two preferences a person has by asking them: Why did you choose this job? Why did you choose your particular house?

External/Internal

You might be able to tell when you've done a good job at work if the boss pats you on the back or tells you, "Good job!" Maybe you've received some award and you get to hang it on your wall for you and everyone else to see. When you receive some physical evidence that you've done a good job, then you yourself can call it a good job. This is called an external preference.

If you had an internal preference, you would seemly feel that you've done a good job. You might win awards for designing an advertising campaign that made a lot of money and even launched you to a higher position in your office, but if you didn't feel it was a good campaign, then awards and more money couldn't convince you otherwise.

Children have an external frame of reference since they absorb the conscious and unconscious teachings of their parents, teachers, and peers. Maturity will then lend itself to shift the child's preference to one that is more internal as he or she develops a better understanding of him or herself. Still he or she may continue to be affected dramatically by outside sources if they have an external preference. The root of this metaprogram is whether the location for motivating yourself and making decisions lies within you or with other people.

In rapport, you can use the internal or external preferences to praise or give feedback or influence simply by recognizing the preferences of the person with whom you are talking. If you are an employer and have an internal frame of reference, make sure to give written or verbal directions or commentary since some of your employees might have external preferences and are feeling neglected. When speaking to a person who operates internally, you might want to use phrases such as "it's entirely up to you," or "see for yourself" to allow them to feel in control and able to judge the situation. If you are speaking to a person who has an external preference, use phrases such as "the top opinion is," or "as studies have proven ..."

In order to figure out if a person has an internal or external preference, you can use these elicitation questions: How do you know when you have been successful at something? How do you know when you've done a good job? Who is responsible for the quality of your work?

Global/Detail

Picture yourself ready to take on the task of the ever-relentless, project of projects, the mighty, intrusive, headache: the cleaning of the bedroom closet. Pretend (or maybe you don't have to pretend) that you haven't done this in years. Pretend that there are heaps of who knows what, things you'd forgotten about, shirts you don't want to remember and shoes that have been walked in and walked over. Each one of these items is now ready for you to decide if it's time for the trash bin, yard sale, or a farewell, adios torching. How do you handle this project? Will you start with the shoes, making two piles of what stays and what doesn't, then move on to the button-down shirts, organizing by color and style? After that, will you move on to the neckties? Or if you are a lady, will you move on to the purse collection? Or would you rather scratch all that and get a big garbage bag and tackle the beast all at once? Would you pick from this shelf and that drawer and toss in or toss about, switching from one side to the other, crouching low, or reaching up high, just to alleviate the grand problem staring right at you?

If you are one of those people who prefer looking at the details and dealing with them bit by bit, you obviously have a *detail* frame of reference. You handle information in sequential steps and often have trouble getting your priorities straight because you cannot seem to generalize connection to other areas with which you are working. These people are best at working with fine details over a period of time, like those in an assembly line or laboratory.

If you prefer tackling the entire beast, you have a global preference and like to consider the bigger picture. You have trouble working with details and when getting ready to deal with a task, you'll want to see a big picture outline to understand just what you'll be getting at.

You could probably think of a particular task that you've had trouble completing due to procrastination. Maybe it's your bedroom closet or maybe it's not. Perhaps it seems like such a huge task that you're simply dreading it and are intimidated by its propensity. Try this process to cut the task into minor bits so that you might tackle each bit at a time.

1.) Stop worrying about it.

2.) Grab a notebook and pen.

3.) Establish a list. Consider and write down what is most important to you about the task.

4.) Rearrange the list in order of importance. You might want to break the list into a series of reasonable actions.

5.) Tackle each action at a time.

To establish if a person prefers a global or detail frame of reference, you can use these questions to elicit: If we were going to work on a project together, would you want to know the big picture first or would you want to get the details of what we're going to do first? What would you prefer to know first: the overall picture or the fine details?

It is important to remember that we combine our metaprograms in different ways depending on which environment we are in. For example, at your job you might combine the metaprograms of *proactive, procedures, details,* and *away from,* but at home you might choose a *reactive, options, global, and toward* while in your comfort zone. In the same sense, different professions require different combinations of metaprograms in order for tasks to be properly and sensibly completed. If you were the head of your own company, it might be most beneficial give all the metaprograms a fair chance since there are probably many people below you with varieties of their own.

In NLP, one of the key techniques of attaining power and success is by studying models. You would look to those who have achieved success and mirror in order to get the same results. However, you don't always have to look to others to mirror and accomplish. You can be a model for yourself. You can look to areas in your own life in which you have great success and mirror the techniques you use there for other areas in your life that lack success. For example, if you are better at getting your children up and ready for school in the morning in record time but cannot seem to check your business voicemails and return all calls fast enough, consider why your morning routine with the children works best and how you can transport those techniques to returning business calls. How do you organize the two separate tasks? Perhaps you are more *proactive*, *towards*, and *procedures* when it comes to getting your children up and going. This may mean that you take on the role as leader, following the same routine, knowing the exact time they should be up and in the shower and dressed and ready with lunches to go. Every component is organized and flows smoothly. The next time you find yourself with a heap of business calls to make, organize them into steps and assign each one with chunks of time in the same way that you would have in the morning. Maybe you can make a list of which calls are more important than others. Or you can divide the list by which ones you think would develop into longer conversations than others. Decide on a time and place to make each call and then make them, working toward the end result of having an abundance of free time to yourself.

Chapter Thirteen:
The Power of
Influence

"The ability to deal with people is as purchasable a commodity as sugar or coffee. And I will pay more for that ability, than for any other under the sun."

—Dale Carnegie

Now you know that good rapport and being able to read someone's body language is a toolbox with much to offer. But once it is open and you know how to master your tools, use them to get what you want. In order to get what you want, you must be powerful enough to be the leader every situation, and being a leader means being able to influence others. Sometimes the briefcase holding a million bucks is open and blaring right before you on the desk. How will you influence the Man to hand it over?

Your ability to influence and persuade others is one of the most important skills not only in the business world, but in many other areas of life as well. You might want your child to do his or her homework without any resistance or complaint. You may want a shopkeeper to lower his or her price for a living room table you can already envision in your house. Whatever the case may be, negotiations are happening in almost every area of your life. You must be able to elicit values and beliefs from the person you are dealing with to acquire a desired state in terms of what you want. We know that beliefs are statements about how we see the world and that they underlie all of our actions and control our behavior. Every aspect of communication is processed through the filter of our beliefs. Our beliefs allow us to do certain things and prevent us from doing others. Beliefs are then linked to values. In an effective communication process, you will work within the other person's belief structure, in their representational systems and metaprograms, which you would have successfully identified in rapport. You must discard your beliefs for a moment and pay full attention to what the other person is telling you. You must be able to see the world through someone else's eyes.

There are two things you want to keep in mind when you want to persuade someone to take an action. First, be laser clear about what you want, or at least the range of outcomes that you want. Second, remember that people do things for their own reasons, not yours. An effective persuader presents strategies and outcomes that are aligned with the other person's values and goals. An idea will be persuasive if its benefits for the other person outweigh its disadvantages. It is often useful to take a few minutes to use a method used by Benjamin Franklin when he was confronted with difficult choices. Write a statement of the proposed course of action at the top of a sheet of paper and draw a line down the middle of the sheet. Write the heading "Pro" on one side and "Con" on the other side. Then on the Pro side list all of the reasons you can think of for the other person to go ahead with a particular course of action. Under Con, list all the reasons for not going ahead. Then consider whether the advantages or the disadvantages have the most weight in term of the other person's values and objectives. This will be effective if you can do this from their perspective, from their model of the world.

Once you have done the analysis and are convinced that you have a good idea from the other person's point of view, your next step is to find the best way to present your idea so that the other person will accept it. Your presentation of the idea must be consistent with the their decision making processes, so that they will find it irresistible. Consider the typical decision strategies that people adopt when making a decision.

Decision Strategies

Typically, people will go through the following steps in making and implementing decisions.

1.) Problem/situation analysis

2.) Generate alternative solutions

3.) Choose the best alternative

4.) Implement the chosen alternative

5.) Monitor the results of the alternative

In all negotiations, you must be able to quickly determine the decision-making strategies employed by the person with whom you are negotiating, the process we all go through in making decisions. Decision-making involves three distinct phases:

1.) Motivation: Here lies the interest in considering making a decision. The person is "deciding to decide."

2.) Decision: Here the motivated person makes a decision.

3.) Verification: Here he or she verifies that his or her decision was a good one.

With regard to the Motivation phase, some people will be motivated by short-term gains or necessity. For example, they may have recently moved into town and urgently need a new home. If you were in the business of real estate or home loans, you would need to pick that up. Other people are motivated by long-range considerations. Perhaps they see a market that is on the increase and they know that if they invest right now, they will make money on their investment. A few people are impulse-motivated. They see their dream home and they want it now.

In the decision phase, some will examine every conceivable alternative, while others need two or three alternatives to choose from, and still others don't need any alternatives. Some require third party opinions and must "talk it over" with someone; others prefer to make decisions by themselves. Certain people need to see every piece of documentation and research they can find, while others are happy with a recommendation from a source they find trustworthy. Some people make decisions very quickly while others require days, weeks, and even months. They may be concerned about how a particular course of action will look in the eyes of others or how others will be affected by the decision; for others this will not be the issue.

At the point of verification, the person will find all possible reasons to justify the decision. People want to remain congruent and want to avoid any sense of dissonance. However, some people will often experience "buyer's remorse." In order to identify a person's decision strategy, you need information about how that person has made similar decisions in the past. Look for the patterns in his or her past decisions and use these patterns in designing their communication strategy.

To identify a person's decision strategy, consider asking the following elicitation questions:

Motivation	What do you want, specifically?
	What has prompted you to consider this decision?
	How have decided what you need?
	What's most important to you about …?
	What's next most important to you about …?

Decision	What factors were most important in your decision to purchase/take/choose your last (similar object/suggestion/plan) ...? How did you reach that decision?
Verification	How did you feel after you decided to ...?

You must pay very close attention to the answers as those will provide you with the keys into the other person's mind and help you close the transaction quickly and elegantly. Information gathering is perhaps the most important component in your relationship with the person. You must allot an appropriate amount of time to this component, consistent with their needs. Not only does information gathering allow you to build rapport with them, but it also empowers you in the persuasion process.

Now that you have identified the person's decision strategy, you have the necessary tools to effectively persuade them. Your job is to use this person's decision strategy patterns to develop your communication approach. Generally, the development of your communication plan is a translation of the person's decision strategy, and it looks like this:

Decision Strategy	Presentation Goal
Motivation	Generate Interest

Decision	Maintain Conviction
Verification	Provide Reassurance

When the person is motivated to make a decision, you will know how to support this motivation, communicate your recommendations and convince him or her to accept your ideas. You will know the steps that they will want to follow in making the decision, and when they verify the decision, you will know how to reassure them that the decision was the right one.

When you are identifying a person's strategies, you need to consider the following:

Amount of time needed to reach a decision: If a person typically takes a long time to reach decisions, you cannot expect him or her to feel comfortable in acting quickly on your proposal. If fast action is required, do all you can to help the person gather as much information as he or she may want. When you are dealing with someone who requires a lot of time to make a decision, establish a deadline in his or her mind. You may say, "I know it is important to take the time to make a decision as important as this, and by January 29, I am sure we will have all the facts to complete this deal. January 29 is the date then."

Amount of information needed to reach a decision: Some people require huge amount of information; others require very little. Once you recognize that a person needs a lot of information, give it to him or her. Support your presentation with sentences such as "the data shows," or "it has been demonstrated," "statistics show that," or "the market trends have been." If the person has a clear vision of a desired outcome and can be convinced by strong logic, present your ideas in ways that dovetail with his or her vision to help support it. Present your ideas to support or enhance their vision.

Number of alternatives: Some people will need to consider every possible alternative; others need only a few. If the person you are talking to requires many alternatives, be prepared and offer those alternatives. While doing so, gently lead them to the alternative you consider best. You may say, "Once you decided to choose the second alternative, you will soon find out that this is the one you are looking for."

Third party endorsements: Some people will decide only if credible third party or parties recommend a particular course of action. In this case, you may want to include a significant third party in the discussions and get them on your side.

Dominant perceptual mode: We learned earlier that people receive and process information in terms of their own representational systems, and the three different ones are the visual, auditory, and kinesthetic. To communicate effectively and thus persuade effectively, you must always be paying attention to which representational system they prefer. Remember always to match their language, pace, speech, maintaining good rapport, and get what you want.

In terms of deletion and distortion, when you are speaking with someone and especially trying to negotiate a deal, you need to consider what they might be leaving out so that you can appeal to every aspect of their decision making process.

Deletion

There is an analogous pattern in human communication. People don't communicate fully. When we listen to someone's statements, they convey only part of their thoughts and feelings. Some concerns and values will be unspoken. To determine fully what they really think, we must ask questions. For example, a person might say, "I am not really sure how this would work out." Hearing this sentence we know that the person is experiencing doubt but we don't know what it is that they are unsure of. Is it making this decision, financial problems, family's approval, etc.? There are many possibilities. When we hear a sentence like this, we must ask, "What specifically are you unsure of?" or "How do you want it to work out?" The person will immediately tell us what his or her concerns may be. Armed with this information, we may redirect our conversation, leading him or her to a resourceful state for a desirable transaction.

Distortion

Distortion is a program we use when we misrepresent the data to ourselves, or in some way "blow it out of proportion." Like deletion, distortion can be beneficial or limiting. For example, a salesman may tell his manager that he's had a lot of good interviews. The manager may interpret this information as a lot of good sales when in reality only interviews occurred. When we visualize an event that has not yet occurred, we are distorting sensory data. If we visualize an event that is positive, distortion is beneficial. In our conversations with other people, we may take a person into the future and help him or her create an attractive future vision.

When a person says things that are inconsistent with the facts and their implications as you have identified them, probe this person's impressions. If the person says, "I can't afford this payment," say: "If I could show you how you can save money on your taxes, and instead use the money purchase the property of your dreams, would you like to find out how you can do it?" In our conversations with other people, we can play the magic genie and grant them whichever attractive visions might benefit them, and consequently us in the process.

Future Pacing

One technique I find particularly useful when negotiating with someone is that of Future Pacing. We already know that pacing is something you do in order to get into alignment with another person. Future Pacing enables you to exercise control over something that might happen in the future. Future Pacing refers to anticipating problems that may arise or objections that the other person might raise, and providing to their solutions in advance. It's about thinking ahead.

For example, you might have a client named Jeffrey who you think might later regret his decision. You can say: "Jeffrey, in my experience, some clients have questions that arise naturally later on. If any questions arise for you, what I would like you to do is reach for the phone (here stimulate reaching for a phone) and do not hesitate to give me a call. I will be glad to do whatever needs to be done." By saying this, you have future-paced your client. If Jeffrey feels any kind of "buyer's remorse," he is more likely to call you for reassurance than to cancel the deal.

NLP gives us a practical four-section guideline that we could easily follow in every negotiation. They are composed of Planning, Opening Negotiations, Exchanging, and Closing.

The Planning Process:

1.) Determine your outcome/goal.

2.) Develop as many options as possible to achieve that outcome. Avoid a fixed position. Define upper and lower limits of range.

3.) Identify potential areas of agreement.

4.) Identify issues to be resolved and plan how to discuss them.

5.) Determine your best alternative to an agreement.

Opening the Negotiations:

1.) Establish rapport.

2.) Get consensus that there is basis for negotiation.

3.) Establish the other negotiator's outcome/goal.

The Exchange:

1.) State areas of agreement.

2.) Anchor each and every state that you can utilize later on.

3.) State issues to be resolved.

4.) Probe for others' outcomes in areas of disagreement.

5.) Develop a set of options that include both parties' outcomes. Remind the other of shared interests (commonalities). Ask for help in developing options. Ask for preference among several options. Emphasize objective standards for selecting an option.

Closing:

Summarize your agreement and action plan, emphasizing the next step. Be sure to include who will do what and when they will do it.

Negotiation Tactics to Follow Faithfully

Firstly, never respond to a proposal with a counter proposal. This is an annoying situation for both parties that will never be resolved. Instead, restate, validate, clarify, and probe. Give answers to questions. This is a basic rule. Also be sure to invent options for mutual gain. In other words, make it a win/win situation, one that is not easy to refuse. Remember the law of reciprocity.

Always avoid attacking or defense exchanges! Use the agreement frame: I appreciate, I agree, I respect. You can always appreciate/respect a person's intentions or feelings on an issue, even if you don't agree. Treat your proposal the same way. If attacked, probe for their outcome behind the attack. Remember, it's only information, so don't take it personally.

In rapport, avoid judgments and statements that glorify the options you favor. They will only break rapport and irritate the other person or people. Instead, label suggestions and questions. You can say, "Let me offer a suggestion," or "I'd like to ask a question." Be sure to use "I" statements rather than the accusing "You" statements. Use "I'm having trouble understanding this," rather than "You're not making yourself clear."

Always state your reasons first before making a proposal. Use the "because" frame. "I deserve this because I have worked hard." And be flexible. Minimize the reasons you give when you state an opinion. Multiple reasons give the person the opportunity to select the weakest option and make it the basis for rejecting the option.

Make it point to test the understanding and summarize so that you and the other person are on the same concise path. Use phrases such as: "So you think that ..." and "Your main concern is ..." and "Let me be sure I understand where we are now."

The last negotiation tactic to be followed is to *never* negotiate with yourself in front of another. If there is any objection and you need more information, break or schedule another appointment or session. If you get stuck, stop what you are doing (do something different), generate at least three options and pick the best one. If someone objects to your proposal, ignore it and simply absorb. Restate, using the agreement frame. Align and redirect. Resolve the objection with exaggeration or a conditional close: "How can we solve this concern/issue?" or "What would happen if we resolve this?" using future pacing to jump ahead and take care of any future issues in the present that you control.

Strategies for Influencing People

Once you have discovered someone's strategies in communicating, you can use them as a framework for relaying information back to them, conscientiously using the specific steps of their strategy. If you are trying to motivate your teenage daughter to do her homework, consider a strategy that she would be more likely to adopt. Start with a question, perhaps: How do you motivate yourself in volleyball? Then watch her eye movements and apply the techniques we learned earlier about reading the eyes. If your question elicited the response of her eyes moving to the left when she enthusiastically describes what her teammates tell themselves before they go out to play and then her eyes move to he bottom left when she describes how she reassures herself to win you can pick up what representational systems she prefers. She prefers auditory stimulation so you can help her to become enthusiastic when listening about topics that pertain to her homework and reassuring herself that she will be able to complete such and such task despite how difficult it may seem at the time. You can also influence her to be more consistent with her homework in describing in detail and with enthusiasm the vast rewards of doing her homework, which you can set up however you wish.

Peak Performer

If you are able to master the negotiation process with anyone, you will find yourself in the position of being a peak performer. A peak performer is generally someone who has achieved a high level of mastery or success. As a peak performer you are a model for excellence and inspire other people to follow by your example. Just like Colonel Sanders' chicken recipe, which has been duplicated in all the Kentucky Fried Chicken Restaurants, you have a recipe on how you continue being a top performer just like all the other masters of excellence. In fact that is the recipe for NLP, the accumulation of recipes for all those who have achieved greatness! Here is the recipe:

Attributes, behaviors and strategies:

- ✓ They code their goals (outcomes) in a way that motivated them to action.
- ✓ Translate vision into action.
- ✓ Monitor progress daily.

✓ Utilize others to achieve their vision.

✓ Nurture positive beliefs.

✓ "I and my ideas are worthwhile."

✓ "There is no failure, only feedback."

✓ "In adversity are the seeds of victory."

✓ "I am responsible for my own outcomes."

✓ "Things don't get better by accident-they get better by appropriate action."

✓ "It is not necessary to understand everything to be able to use everything."

Use a specific decision-making strategy

Peak performers visually construct the end result. They start out by deciding and visualizing what they ultimately want to achieve. They talk to themselves about how the end result will benefit them and others. They test their feelings about the respective benefits and costs related to the end result. If the overall feeling is not good, they adapt the content of the end result until it not only feels good, but *great*.

CHAPTER FOURTEEN: LOVE AND NLP

"Sometimes I wonder if men and women really suit each other. Perhaps they should just live next door and visit now and then."

—*Katherine Hepburn*

Mr. And Mrs. Right. Who are these two and more importantly, where have they been hiding? Many men and women have a distinct image in their head of what their supposed soul mate looks like, talks like, walks like, etc. They grow up watching fairy tale cartoons of Prince Charming or comic book sketches of Wonderwoman, fantasizing about unreal characters in books and movies or gawking at someone else's love story, in the process, concocting their ideal someone who they eventually will love someday. Does this sound familiar? Maybe you're thinking about your ideal person right now. Many times, you will fixate on this ideal, obsess about it, wait for it, and develop a strategy in order for you to be truly loved—by this ideal person. Then one day something extraordinary happens. This person, this obsession, this soul mate struts into your life and you are able to exclaim to yourself, "Yes! Finally! I've found *the one!*" They seem to have just all the qualities you were looking for—they are good looking, sweet talking, funny, charming, smart, honest … perfect. You automatically feel fulfilled, you start telling yourself that you've found "love" and immediately begin to project onto your future the fillings of a happy life together. Then something else happens.

Maybe your relationship is months in. Maybe it's a couple of years. Whether it's sooner or later, eventually everything just seems to fall apart and it seems that this soul mate of yours, this ideal person, this lover, no longer meets your par. Somehow your connection is lost, you no longer understand each other, your communication seems to be in trouble, you no longer feel loved or appreciated enough, and you feel something has gone terribly wrong. You begin to question yourself: What did I do wrong? You question him or her: Maybe he (or she) doesn't love me anymore!

One reason that NLP gives us for this common, everyday tragedy is that you and your ideal person have simply reverted back to who you both really are. When you meet someone you like and find interesting, you will usually woo him or her by firing off all the modalities, or representational systems at once. And they will do the same with you. Remember that modalities are the visual, auditory and kinesthetic frames of reference that we prefer. You will appeal to the other person's visual modality by making an effort to look good. You will wear the color they like and they will wear the color you like. You will appeal to their auditory modality by speaking softly and saying the things he or she wants to hear. You will appeal kinesthetically by touching them often, playing with their hair, holding hands, kissing, being as affectionate as possible so that they know how much you care about them. If they respond with the same efforts, it doesn't take long before the two of you are completely hooked on one another. You have appealed to all the modalities and in the process clicked with the one or two that the other person prefers as they have done the same with you.

However, in due time, you become yourself again and start to operate in the modality you usually work in and they start operating in theirs and you feel something has been lost. No longer do you hear the loving phrases and pet names you used to adore (you being auditory, he or she not being). Meanwhile, they might be just as easily thinking to themselves: "Why doesn't she hold my hand the way she used to?" This is because they are kinesthetic while you are not.

Sometimes to find out what modality your person prefers can be as easy as asking a simple question: What would make you feel more loved? You can precede this question by stating the obvious (if it is true, of course): You know I love you, right? You can use the techniques that we learned in Chapter Five by following their eyes to access their strongest modality. If the person's eyes move to the horizontal left (auditory remembered), ask what sorts of things he or she might like to hear or do the work yourself and think about what things you have said in the past that have made them particularly happy. If their eyes move to the bottom right (kinesthetic), try initiating more physical contact, kissing more, holding hands, or using any other touch you might think they would enjoy. If you really wanted to walk through this blindly and not do any research, you could obviously fire off all modalities just as you did when you were wooing them, but of course this could be an exhausting option, so just do the research!

Rules

Another key to maintaining a successful relationship is to understand what rules the other person has constructed so that you can choose to either adhere to them or bring them to the table to challenge them. For example, a woman might complain to her husband that he does not love her because he does not spend enough time with her and the family since he is always at work. However, in the husband's mind, the reason he is at work all the time is because he wants a better life with his family and because he loves them and wants to give them everything they want. Meanwhile, the husband and wife have two separate perceptions of what love constitutes, regardless of the fact that they both profess love. It is entirely possible and plausible that two people could love each other but have different perceptions of what love is. If their relationship continues this way without communicating what their perception entails, they are likely to end up in divorce. Rules in relationships are determined by a person's previous relationships with other people. Once you set a rule and the other person breaks it, there is conflict in the relationship. Add that to working in separate modalities, and you will never be able to communicate which rule has been broken and how and why you work the way that you do. Conflicts will only get bigger and bigger with little or no communication until your relationship ends in disaster.

The following chart is an example of conflicting rules in a relationship to help you find ones that might furtively exist in yours. The scenario is husband and wife, where he is employed and she runs the household. (Of course the scenario can be easily swapped for the wife as the one who is employed and the husband as head of household.)

HIS	HERS
He should be able to go out with friends once a week	He should not need his friends to be happy
He needs to relax when he comes home from work	If he cared, he would talk to her when he comes home from work
He wants to enjoy his hobbies when he is off work	She wants to still be taken out on dates
She should have a meal set for him when he comes home from work	He should help out around the house when he comes home from work

She should be in charge of the household bills	He should offer to help with the bills since they both share the expenses
He shouldn't have to return phone calls right away if he is busy at work	He should be considerate enough to return phone calls to his loved ones right away
She should be in charge of the children's home-work and extracurricular activities	He should take an active part in his children's lives

The key to distinguishing rules in a relationship: Communication! This cannot be stressed enough. Ask questions to figure out what the rules are, what modalities your husband and wife prefers, and what you can do to show you care. It is really that simple. Understand and appreciate the different shapes and sizes of perception.

Submodalities and Relationships

We learned earlier that submodalities are the subclassifications of external experience. For instance, a picture has brightness, depth, distance, and size. A sound has volume, tone, pitch, etc. By using our submodalities, we are able to manipulate the experience to make it either more enjoyable or less powerful (if it was a bad experience). We can use submodalities in the same sense when dealing with our romantic relationships.

Try this. Visualize your loved one in front of you in the state that you have seen them most happy and one in which you enjoy seeing them. Intensify this image of them by having them smile and brightening their features. Imagine that they are radiating with a magnificent glow. Bring them closer to you in the image, making them bolder and bigger and more vibrant and pleasing an image. Brighten the image more and as you brighten it, imagine him or her smiling even wider, perhaps even laughing so that you can hear them loud and clear. Ask yourself when and where have you enjoyed their voice most. What elements about their voice enabled your enjoyment? Were they speaking slowly and gently? Or was their voice high pitched and cheery? What tone did they use? Use whichever elements worked and apply them to your visual image to produce an entirely pleasurable image. Allow yourself to feel just as happy as your loved one appears in your mind. If you feel comfortable enough, share with your loved one your practice with submodalities and note their response. They might be pleased and attempt the same practice. All you are doing is intensifying the experience you share with him or her by appreciating the minute details of what actually constitutes the experience—sights, sounds and feelings.

You can also manipulate submodalities to let go of a time when you had a bad experience with your husband or wife since this experience might still be the source of a continuing grudge or unresolved conflict. Think of a time when you were both having an argument. Where did it happen? How did it sound? What were you telling each other and how did it feel? Be as specific as possible. Use either the swish method to swap this experience with another, more pleasing one, or simply change the submodalities and focus in on the changes to change your emotional association with the experience. Change the tone, distance, and lighting of the experience. If you were having the argument outdoors on a sunny day, change the image into one that is black and white and if you were shouting at each other, lower the voices into gentle whispers. Make the experience slow motion as well. What happens to your feelings as you change these features of the event? It should be less intensified.

Together you can experiment with submodalities to intensify your experience in pleasurable ways with one another. You can work on kinesthetic submodalities by changing the pressure and pace of kissing or even the elements that go into holding hands. Talking about and changing even the simplest experiences can result in incredible rewards. You can turn something ordinary into something so gratifying with the littlest effort just because you are playing with it and mixing things up. Talk to your husband and wife to find out what submodalities they would like to experiment with; just asking is sometimes enough effort to reignite a spark that seems to somehow have been lost.

Anchoring and Relationships

In NLP, anchoring is used to describe the mind's inclination to associate two unrelated experiences by a single emotion. We talked earlier about transforming negative beliefs about ourselves through anchoring. In this section, we will learn how to transform negative beliefs about our loved one through anchoring and implementing positive beliefs instead. We can apply anchoring to relationships when we begin to realize how our actions and the actions of our partners can place anchors into our own emotional experience, resulting in links that we may not have intended to create. For example, if you came home ecstatic by a promotion you'd just received and see your partner's face, you will unconsciously link your ecstatic feeling with the plain sight of his or her face. In a more negative light, if you hated your job and always talked about it with him or her, you would begin to associate the negative feelings about your job with him or her whether you mean to or not.

This is why it is ever important to share good experiences and events in which you cherish with your partner so that you will associate positive feelings with the sight of them. This creates positive anchors with the simplest effort of just sharing your positive news. I don't mean that you should not ever share your bad days or experiences with your loved one, just practice the sharing of good news more frequently. The build-up of too many negative anchors and your association of negativity to your loved ones are sometimes the only causes for divorce and breaking up.

Use anchoring to conscientiously improve your relationship in areas that matter most. Make an effort to plan positive events together and keep them entirely positive! If for some reason you feel an argument starting to brew, interfere and make the bold decision to have the argument later. This will keep you from turning a positive event into a negative one and chances are you will both forget about what the argument would have been. During this positive event, if you come across an intensely positive moment you are sharing, anchor the event by touching your partner on the arm or putting your arms around him or her so that the next time you make this gesture somewhere else, you will re-access the positive feelings in which it was first initiated.

Just be careful in using anchoring because it can just as easily produce negative effects. If you give your husband a watch after purposefully provoking an argument and saying cruel things that you regretted later, he will only think of this argument and your cruel words every time he checks the time. Never use gifts by way of apology because this gift will only be an anchor for negative feelings. Save gifts for positive events and drop anchors as frequently as you can. Don't give up on your relationship unless you have researched everything. Have you researched everything? Start asking questions immediately!

PART THREE:
FEEL DIFFERENT

CHAPTER FIFTEEN: THE PHILOSOPHY OF BREATH

"For breath is life, and if you breathe well you will live long on Earth."

—*Sanskrit Proverb*

Now that we understand how incredibly powerful the mind is and how our positive thoughts can lead to positive action and the manifestation of our wildest dreams, let's zoom out and partake in a different discussion. As far as our dreams are concerned, our mental health is virtually useless if we do not have physical health to support it. In fact, if we were mentally unhealthy, our physical states would be in trouble too. That is because the two components go hand in hand. One component cannot thrive without the other. And you cannot thrive if you are not taking care of both. Let's start with the most fundamental detail of our physical wellness: the breath.

Breath is the essence of life. It is the aerobic organism's necessity and the primary link between you and success. How? We may know less about breath than we think. When was the last time you took a full one? If you have ever taken any yoga classes, you might already be well on you way to breathing well and thus living well. In order to be fully present and capable of success, the elements in your body must be flowing easily and abundantly or you will begin to wither away in exhaust and inactivity. Most of us deny ourselves full breaths. Either we are too busy to even consider them or too inclined to sigh instead. For whatever reason we choose to deny ourselves full breaths, by doing so we deny ourselves a full life in the process.

There is a whole philosophy to breath. We know that the purpose of breathing is to get oxygen from the air into our bodies. The organs we use are the mouth, nose, gult, windpipe, lungs, and diaphragm. Oxygen also gets rid of waste products such as carbon dioxide. Every cell in your body needs oxygen to function. Brain cells are particularly sensitive to oxygen and they will start dying if they do not have oxygen for as little as four minutes[7]. Oxygen content changes in the brain will alter

---

7   Kamler, *Surviving the Extremes: A Doctor's Journey to the Limits of Human Endurance*, 90.

the way a person feels and behaves. A person who is angry will have a different breathing pattern than a person who is not angry. An angry person will breathe shallower and significantly faster. A shallower breathing pattern is inefficient, and the oxygen content in the angry person's blood is lowered[8]. Less oxygen to the brain will make a person more irritable, confused, and more likely to demonstrate negative behavior such as yelling, threatening and fighting.

Breathing not oxygenates cells, but it also controls the flow of lymph fluid, which contains white blood cells, which protect the body. Every cell in our body is surrounded by lymph fluid, which acts as a sewage system for a cell, taking oxygen and nutrients necessary from blood and excreting toxins in the process. This entire process is activated by deep breathing. Without deep breathing and without this process, we would never be able to get rid of harmful toxins and absorb the nutrients we need to create energy and preserve our cells. Most of us are unaware of this so we hold on to so much excess waste, inhibiting our potential for having full health.

Ninety-nine percent of a person's energy should come from breathing yet most of us breathe at only 10 to 20 percent of our potential. Optimal breathing gets you more vitality and better quality of life. It is not the only component to getting

8   Nay, *Taking Charge of Anger*, 34.

healthy and maintaining health, but it is a fundamental part. The average person reaches peak respiratory function and lung capacity in their mid-twenties. Then they begin to lose 10 to 27 percent of respiratory capacity for every decade of life[9]. The only way to improve and maintain proper respiratory function is to learn how to breathe well.

The key to beginning to breathe properly is to follow these steps:

1.) Close your eyes.

2.) Put one hand on your belly and the other on your chest.

3.) For a few minutes, feel the rhythm of your breathing.

4.) If you breathe with your chest, you are breathing shallow.

5.) If you breathe with your belly, you are breathing correctly.

The way you breathe has a huge impact on how you feel every sensation and how efficiently your motor skills function.

---

9   Cotes, *Lung Function: Physiology, Measurement and Application in Medicine*, 318.

A baby almost exclusively breathes with its belly. Most adults breathe almost totally from the upper chest.

Most people believe that the reason people smoke is because of all the nicotine that they are addicted to in the cigarettes. This is not true. This might be the reason they pick up the cigarette and make the habitual movement from hand to mouth, but that is not the reason they enjoy the cigarette. When a person smokes, they take deep breaths. There is more oxygen going through the blood and they consequently feel relaxed. When they are stressed, people that smoke typically run out to have a cigarette. As soon as they are done smoking, they feel good. This is not due to the smoke but because they were breathing through their bellies. You can achieve the same high and alter your mood just as efficiently without the toxic effects of cigarettes. You can do it with the nourishing effects of oxygen.

Another way you can get recharged is to follow these steps:

1.) Inhale as many full breaths as you can until your lungs can't take any more air.

2.) Hold your breath until you can't hold it anymore.

3.) Exhale slowly.

4.) You will feel tingles all over your body. That is the oxygen being pumped into your blood stream and your brain.

5.) Every time you feel stressed or sluggish, this practice will make you feel recharged. Try it!

Some other interesting facts about breath is that in Tai Chi Chuan, aerobic training is combined with breathing to exercise the diaphragm muscles and to install effective posture, both beneficial for generating energy in our bodies. In the practice of meditation, specifically anapana and other forms of yoga, the breath is brought to one's consciousness and full breaths are practiced thoroughly so that your mind and body will make a habit of bringing full breathing to your everyday living. The phenomenon of laughter is physically composed of taking sharp, repeated breaths.

Our optimal natural states should be clear-headed and refreshed in the mornings, vitalized and energized throughout our day, possessing good memory and positive thoughts, and always capable of taking a full breath. So indulge! But breathe easily and without straining. Remember that the ideal respiration is deep, slow, silent and easy. Always be good to your lungs, your minds, and yourself.

CHAPTER SIXTEEN: THE SECRET TO CREATING ENERGY

"A person of intellect without energy added to it is a failure."

—*Sebastien-Roch Nicolas De Chamfort*

Energy, in physics, is described as the amount of work a physical system can do on another. A conventional definition of energy is the capacity to do work. Either way, you are seeing that word "work" and considering a definition for that word alone. Work, not just your "job," not just your exercise regimen, not just your household chores, is the essence of doing something. Without energy, you would never be able to do a single thing. In fact, your whole being can be looked at as one large unit or an accumulation of various smaller units of energy and the world outside of you is another field of energy and what you do with your energy in relation to the outside world is just another unit of this thing. All is energy. Energy, in the sense of this chapter, is more specifically the fuel of action and the hence the fuel of manifesting excellence.

Learning to breathe well is the beginning source of being able to put our minds in the right state to take care of our bodies. We know breathing oxygenates the cells and the cells nourish our whole state of being. You should already begin to feel vitalized feeding your lungs and cells with deep, healthy breathing. Now you will uncover the truth about sleep and the science of exercise as contributing factors to your overall health ... and success.

Breathing, sleep, exercise, foods and drink all contribute to the overall health of your body so that it can be fueled enough to manifest the excellent life your mind dreams up. Your mind and your body vigorously depend on each other and need to be aligned in order to even dream up excellent things and what aligns them is energy. You can work on changing your internal representations for years but if you live your life in exhaust or malnourishment, your brain will only continue to create mis-representations. You can read a thousand books about striving, about achieving, about believing, but it will go unused if your body is too de-energized to reach for that one pivotal factor on which all of this information relies: Action. Without the fuels of breathing, sleep, exercise and wholesome food and drink, you will have no energy to even consider action. You will remain in the repetitive cycles of "I'll use this information one day," when you are less tired and less hungry and more inclined to get up and change. Change today. Use this information as your reason.

The Truth about Sleep

So it was a late night out. It started with a heavy dinner at that new Italian place in town, then moved on to the latest action-packed flick at the theater, and ended with couple of nightcaps at the local bar. By the time you got home, you knew you'd be sorry in the morning when you would have to be up early for work. Sure enough, having only slept a measly five hours with most of it spent tossing and turning over the thought of your upcoming day, you woke up at the farthest, dreadfully ruthless wrong side of the bed. How well do you know that side of the bed?

Sleep. It is the state of natural rest observed by most mammals, birds and fish. In humans and in many other animals that have been studied, regular sleep is necessary for survival. But of what does "regular sleep" actually consist? Before the invention of the light bulb, it was estimated that a typical adult slept over 9 hours each night. New studies show that an infant averages 14 hours of sleep, while an adult now averages 7.5 each night. A senior adult surpasses that with an average of a whopping 16 hours. Talk about being refreshed!

However, the length of sleep is not what causes us to be refreshed upon waking. The key is the number of complete sleep cycles we enjoy. Each sleep cycle contains five distinct phases that exhibit different wave patterns.

a.) Pre-sleep: normal alertness

b.) Phase 1 sleep: the mind at rest, eyes closed, breathing slowed, images are beginning to appear; these images can be voluntarily controlled since you are still conscious at this point

c.) Phase 2 sleep: light sleep

d.) Phase 3 sleep: deep sleep

e.) Phase 4 sleep: rapid eye movement (REM) sleep, or dreaming

f.) Phase 5 sleep: light sleep, signaling the end of a cycle

An average cycle of sleep can be as short as 90 minutes, which gives the practice of naps much prestige. The REM phase is estimated to be as short as 20 minutes with normal sleep being at 65 minutes of normal sleep before the dream and 5 minutes afterward. Alcohol, overeating, and/or medication can shorten the REM phase and lessen your quality of sleep which was the case in the above scenario with a heavy Italian meal, a couple of nightcaps and an abundance of tossing and turning.

It really doesn't matter whether you sleep twelve hours tonight or five. The physical and mental benefits of sleep will only be produced by how many complete sleep cycles you experienced. If you fall asleep within five minutes of setting your head on the pillow, then most likely you are suffering from exhaust. The typical waiting period between lying in bed and falling asleep is around 15 to 20 minutes. If you can't fall asleep within 15 or 20 minutes, don't resort to popping a pill; simply trust that you're not tired! Within the rules of moderation, it has been said to eat when you're hungry, drink when you're thirsty, and go to sleep when you're sleepy. If you follow these rules, you are sure to awaken with refreshment and clarity every morning, en route to making every day a productive one.

The Science of Exercise

Yoga. Pilates. Running. Biking. Aerobics. Weightlifting. Whatever your exercise is, the basic fundamental it boils down to is movement. When your body is rested and nourished enough, you will be more inclined to move. As you awaken movement for your body, your thoughts will be just as inclined to move from a negative thought to a positive one. Your physiology can help you produce outstanding results. One of the most important things that physical movement provides us with is an abundant focus on breath. We already discussed the philosophy of breath in the first chapter so you know that your entire system depends upon it. Consider this: why do athletes experience a dramatically lower cancer rate than average, non-athletic Americans? This is because athletes are constantly oxygenating their cells. They are also stimulating their bodies' immune systems as a result of stimulating their lymph system with constant deep breathing. Yoga is one of the most effective systems at bringing your consciousness to deep, healthy breathing. The word "aerobic" literally means: to exercise with air. Any aerobic exercise will utilize the breath along with swimming as well.

After a powerful session of running or biking or performing whatever exercise activity you like best, you might find that you are not hungry for a heavy, fatty, unhealthy meal. The bodily stimulation and constant high-pumped oxygenation of your cells has already provided you with as much nourishment and energy that a meal might. You will be satisfied enough to make better choices for meals when your body is functioning on its optimal level. Not only that, but regular exercise will also build up your immune system which is our body's natural agent for fighting disease and infection.

Frequent and regular exercise has been shown to decrease serious and often fatal diseases such as high blood pressure, obesity, heart disease, Type 2 diabetes[10], and will even help to elevate the symptoms of depression. Exercise will not only contribute to creating fuel or energy, but it will also help raise a person's threshold for what they consider "pain." If kept up, a person who exercises on a regular basis and is in an optimal state of health will often increase the body's natural creation of endorphins, an opiate that in conjunction with other neurotransmitters will produce the exercise-induced euphoria. If exercise has never felt *that* good, then try it again or until it does. Enter into your dream diary "Appointment: To experience exercise-induced euphoria." It is scientifically proven you will know just how this feels. Consider it research.

---

10   Hoeger and Hoeger, *Lifetime Physical Fitness and Wellness: A Personalized Program*, 298.

Chapter Seventeen:
Food for Thought

"To eat is a necessity, but to eat intelligently is an art."

—La Rochefoucauld

When you're looking to obtain a healthy body, think of your cells. The most invaluable thing to remember about living health is the breath, as we have consistently discussed thus far. The more oxygen you breathe in, the stronger your cells become, and the more energy you will have as a result. When cells are exposed to something they shouldn't, our bodies are more prone to receive diseases. Bad habits are what lead to toxins collecting in your bloodstream. Germs or Microbes do not necessarily signify disease. Medical research does show that you can have germs or viruses in your body even if you are healthy. It is a combination of germs, viruses, and the toxicity level in your body that causes diseases and illnesses. When your body is at alkaline level, meaning your pH is above 7 you will be *more resistant* to all diseases/illnesses. The complete opposite is true, if your body is below 7, you are more likely to get a disease/illness. Some ways to ensure that your pH level is above 7 and that you will create energy and maintain health enlist these things in your life:

1.) Breathe

2.) Alkaline water and food

3.) Aerobic exercise and strength

4.) Proper diet

5.) Positive mindset

6.) Disposing of processed fats

7.) Disposing of dairy products

8.) Disposing of addictions with acids

With seventy percent of the planet made up of water and eighty percent of our bodies also made up of water, it's obvious how important it is to persistently feed our bodies with this substance. This can be fulfilled not just by drinking water, but also by consuming water-rich foods.

Although drinking water is fundamental, it is unnecessary to drink more than eight or nine glasses if you are not thirsty. And when we do drink water, we should be drinking alkaline water, which we will discuss further in a few moments. Water-rich foods are basically fruits, vegetables and sprouts. These will provide you with a tremendous amount of water as well as help satiate your hunger and assist in cleansing you of harmful toxins built up in your system. Most people, if they have not used a colon cleanse or if they do not ingest a healthy intake of water-rich foods and alkaline water, live their entire lives with an enormous build-up of toxic waste products, which eventually lead to disease. Why do you think heart disease is one of our biggest killers? Where did this come from? Inability to eliminate.

The following is a list of **Alkalizing Foods** so that you can align your pH levels to a healthy state.

Vegetables	Garlic, Asparagus, Fermented, Veggies, Watercress, Beets, Broccoli, Brussel Sprouts, Cabbage, Carrots, Cauliflower, Celery, Chard, Chlorella, Collard Greens, Cucumbers, Eggplant, Kale, Kohlrabi, Lettuce, Mushrooms, Mustard Greens, Dulce, Dandelions, Edible Flowers, Onions, Parsnips, Peas, Peppers, Pumpkin, Rutabaga, Sea Veggies, Spirulina, Sprouts, Squashes, Alfalfa, Barley Grass, Wheat Grass, Wild Greens
Fruits	Apples, Apricots, Avocados, Bananas, Cantaloupes, Cherries, Currants, Dates/Figs, Grapes, Grapefruits, Limes, Honeydew, Melons, Nectarines, Oranges, Lemons, Peaches, Pears, Pineapple, All Berries, Tangerine, Tomato, Tropical Fruits, Watermelon

244 Mind's Power Unleashed

Protein	Eggs, Whey Protein, Powder, Cottage Cheese, Chicken Breast, Yogurt, Almonds, Chestnuts, Tofu, Flax Seeds, Pumpkin Seeds, Squash Seeds, Sunflower Seeds, Millet, Sprouted Seeds, Nuts
Other	Apple Cider Vinegar, Bee Pollen, Lecithin Granules, Probiotic Cultures, Green Juices, Veggie Juices, Fresh Fruit Juices, Organic Milk (unpasteurized), Mineral Water, Alkaline Antioxidant, Water, Green Tea, Herbal Tea, Dandelion Tea, Ginseng Tea, Banchi Tea, Kombucha
Sweeteners	Stevia
Spices/ Seasonings	Cinnamon, Curry, Ginger, Mustard, Chili Peppers, Sea Salt, Miso, Tamari, Herbs
Oriental Vegetables	Maitake, Daikon, Dandelion Root, Shitake, Kombu, Reishi, Nori, Umeboshi, Wakame, Sea Veggies

The following is a list of **Acidifying Foods:**

Fats & Oils	Avocado Oil, Canola Oil, Corn Oil, Hemp Seed Oil, Flax Oil, Lard, Olive Oil, Safflower Oil, Sesame Oil, Sunflower Oil
Fruits	Cranberries
Grains	Rice Cakes, Wheat Cakes, Amaranth, Barley, Buckwheat, Corn, Oats (rolled), Quinoi, Rice (all), Rye, Spelt, Kamut, Wheat, Hemp Seed, Flour
Dairy	Cheese, Cow Cheese, Goat Cheese, Processed Cheese, Milk, Butter
Nuts & Butters	Cashews, Brazil Nuts, Peanuts, Peanut Butter, Pecans, Tahini, Walnuts
Animal Protein	Beef, Carp, Clams, Fish, Lamb, Lobster, Mussels, Oyster, Pork, Rabbit, Salmon, Shrimp, Scallops, Tuna, Turkey, Venison
Pasta (White)	Noodles, Macaroni, Spaghetti
Other	Distilled Vinegar, Wheat Germ, Potatoes
Drugs & Chemicals	Chemicals, Medicinal Drugs, Psychedilic Drugs, Pesticides, Herbicides
Alcohol	Beer, Spirits, Hard Liquor, Wine

Beans & Legumes	Black Beans, Chick Peas, Green Beans, Kidney Beans, Lentils, Lima Beans, Pinto Beans, Red Beans, Soy Beans, Soy Milk, White Beans, Rice Milk, Almond Milk

During the average person's aging process, acid waste develops throughout the body. Most will be disposed through your bowels, kidneys, and even liver. Unfortunately, when our bodies won't rid of acid waste easily enough, it will store itself in our organs (heart, colon, liver.)

To have a healthy natural life, your body needs to contain more alkaline fluid—where the pH is higher than 7.0 (extremely clean water). One of the best things you can do to live a healthier life is drink alkaline water. Just because it's in a bottle, doesn't mean it's alkaline. The water that comes from snow melting into mountain lakes and streams is considered the best quality water available on the planet. Alkaline water won't be the easiest thing for you to find, but it will definitely be worth the effort when you notice the overall change in your health.

Another thing to avoid is the growth of Candida in your body. Candida is a fungus that potentially can lead to diseases such as AIDS, allergies, fatigue, herpes, and many others. It simply eats the body away and destroys your immune system. It starts out as yeast and then eventually attacks the cells in your body. The main focus of this parasite is the already weaker cells changing your physiology.

Twenty years ago, it was rare to have Candida. Now it is found in over 50 percent of he people across the United States and Canada[11]. Having Candida in your body is one more way to keep your body away from alkaline level.

Diseases start by autointoxication, ways in which we induce ourselves with toxins by knowingly taking poisons (illegal drugs as well as most legal pharmaceuticals and chemicals) to destroy your body. Herbs and holistic healing products may be more expensive but are certainly healthier and more effective for your body. Another method of autointoxication is a bad diet and having your blood stream at the pH level of acidic. Lastly, diseases can be just as easily caused by negative thoughts, which cause you to fall short of breath, tense up, and hold onto your body's bulk of waste products. Dr. Andrew Weil M.D. from Harvard, also author of *Health and Healing* says it best when he talks about focusing on building a more resistant body than fighting the disease agents. So do what you can now to strengthen your body and live healthily, instead of

---

11   Hall, *Healthful Eating*, 3.

destructively going about your day, with blind faith in all the products you are surrounded by.

Below is an entertaining list of health beliefs that society wants us to believe in—which are not true:

- ✓ An apple a day will keep the doctor away
- ✓ You'll get sick if you play in the rain
- ✓ Being sick is harmlessly normal
- ✓ Prescription and non-prescription medicine will cure all
- ✓ Antibiotics get rid of the viruses
- ✓ Milk from the grocery store is healthy to drink
- ✓ The sun causes skin cancer
- ✓ Acne comes from eating chocolate and oily foods

Conclusion

"Success is not the key to happiness. Happiness is the key to success."

—*Albert Schweitzer*

We are in an age where living an extraordinary life, having unfaltering success, and owning the ability to manifest anything we can conceive are options available to anyone. However, the only way to access these things is by exhibiting conscious effort. Conscious effort = action. With the bombardment of the world, all the teachings it contains, all the different perceptions and attitudes and "realities" it throws at you, the choice to become a blob of confusion seems easy to you. It seems easy to choose a life of indifference rather than looking inwardly to challenge the thoughts you have lived with for so long. It doesn't matter if they are dismantling, disempowering thoughts that tell you that you don't deserve as much as you want. Modern society makes this choice even easier with its constant clatter, its television stars and pharmaceutical commercials, its capitalist claims that all tell you to live in a life of mediocre uniformity so you will keep buying the same products, keep feeling sad enough to need another one of their pills, keep seeking the same, limiting cycle so that while you don't take a step for greatness, they take another giant leap.

Meanwhile, you forget to take full breaths. You grow angry. You toss and turn, trying to make sense of all this clatter and never get a proper good night's rest. Never mind a nap, you have no time for that. You shop at the same grocery stores which provide you with foods and products pumped up with chemicals that will keep you in a constant state of illness and exhaust—just the right state to make "comfortable" buying choices again. You are too busy and too comfortable in your unhappiness that the thought of living an extraordinary life, the thought of acquiring greatness, the thought of manifesting all you have ever wanted in your life becomes disengaging and unreal. This thought becomes one for another life, for someone more capable, less tired, more charismatic, more bold, one meant for someone with more money, more time, and more choices.

That's not who you are.
Not anymore.

Remember that the mind and body are interlinked and they will always depend on one another. Every thought you have reaches out to the deepest, darkest cell at the very edge of your body with your body's neurotransmitters. Your organs can also produce the same neurotransmitters that are found in the brain and if your organs aren't functioning correctly, your neurotransmitters won't be working correctly. As a result, your cells will not continue being stimulated and nourished. In other words, the cycle will not work. When your mind is burdened with many negative thoughts, it affects your deep limbic system and results in moodiness and symptoms of depression. Teaching yourself to control and direct thoughts in a positive way is one of the most effective ways to easily feel better. Realize and make a conscious effort every day of your life to understand how real your thoughts are and what a tremendous effect they have on your body and life. Break it down into a simple process: you have a thought, this thought releases chemicals, an electrical transmission travels through your brain, you become aware of it, and you behave a certain way because of it. If you can learn to listen to your thoughts, you can learn to control them.

Negative thoughts will always affect your body negatively and produce undesirable conditions. Every time you think of something that provokes anger or sadness, your bran releases chemicals that make your body feel bad. Your muscles tense up, your heart beats fast and uneasy, your hands begin to sweat and you might even feel a bit dizzy. You are putting your body through torment. And for what reason? Something entirely preventable. Make a habit of focusing on the positive aspects of life and don't resort to fortune telling unless you are predicting only the most beautiful things for your life. Disengage guilt and blame and labeling in your life because you will only set yourself up for disappointment and negatively distort your perceptions of other people.

Your mind and body are the greatest instruments on Earth. Why not, in this life here, this same one you've been in since day one, this one that might disappoint you, that you might have been taking for granted, this life that will be over one day in preparation for someone else's story, simply let yourself be happy. Live the life you imagined as a child: a life of excitement, of glory, and of joy. Believe that you deserve greatness. Transform your memories into appreciated moments of growth. Keep asking questions of others and of yourself to uncover what more there can be, what more you can do, how much more you can accomplish just by asking. Be a friend to yourself by not being detrimental to all the voices inside you saying, "Yes! I want that! I want that now!" Sometimes the id is not the worst judge. Be enthusiastic.

Look to the teachers who have left their footprints bold and easy to follow. Use their same words and techniques and believe that you can achieve the same levels of accomplishment and grandeur by living by their doctrines. There is enough evidence to lead your way. Trust it.

Master your equipment, your tools. Know the functions of the brain, reframe your thoughts, and reprogram the software to be rid of the pestering viruses that hold you back. Jump ahead! Use the knowledge of thought processes, of the equipment, to talk to anyone, anywhere, about anything. Be influential. Reap power.

Be good to your body. Breathe in the elements that you give you life so that you may lead an abundant one. Abundant breath gives you an abundance of choices, of possibilities, of dreams and of happiness. Sleep and dream so that when you wake you can realize those dreams. Stretch and run and be active so that physical activity will enable mental activity. Action = Power! Eat foods that will propel you, not hinder you. Let your body be vitalized enough to support your reaching mind. Let your mind keep reaching and be ever receiving. Use my words and this manual and your achieved success as models for your future of everlasting, extraordinary successes to come. Then share with others how they can, too. For there is enough good living to go around for everyone!

Success

To laugh often and much; to win the respect of intelligent people and the affection of children; to earn the appreciation of honest critics and endure the betrayal of false friends; to appreciate beauty, to find the best in others; to leave the world a bit better, whether by a healthy child, a garden patch or a redeemed social condition; to know even one life has breathed easier because you have lived. This is to have succeeded."

—Ralph Waldo Emerson

GLOSSARY

Action: The fact or process of doing something, usually to achieve an aim.

Anchoring: The process by which you any representation triggers a predefined process of thoughts, emotions, and responses. It can be a touch, a smell, a word, a specific name or even a picture, a gesture, or a color. They can be naturally occurring or set up deliberately.

Associated State: In memory, looking through your own eyes to duplicate the same feelings you had at a previous time.

Auditory: Relating to hearing or the sense of hearing.

Away from: A metaprogram. When a person's preference is to move in the opposite direction than what they want.

Beliefs: Closely held generalizations about the world, our identity, meaning, behavior, and capabilities. They are guiding principles or dictums that provide meaning and direction in our life.

Collapsing Anchors: When two separate anchors are released simultaneously, resulting in two different internal experiences.

Communication: The process of conveying information by language, signs, symbols, or behavior. It works toward an outcome.

Cross-over mirroring: Matching a person's body language with a different type of movement. For example: tapping your foot to match their head nods.

Decision: A conclusion or resolution reached after consideration.

Deletion: Parts of your original experience that have been left out of your internal representation. This keeps us from being overburdened with an accumulation of sensory information.

Digital: Having a discrete on/off meaning.

Disassociation: In memory, looking at yourself from the outside so that you do not have the feelings you had then.

Distortion: The process in which things are inaccurately included in a person's internal representation in a limiting way.

Elicitation: Gathering information by direct observation of a person's gestures and language and formulating questions that determine the structure of their internal experience.

Environment: What we perceive as being outside of us. It is the context in which our behavior takes place and something we feel we must react to.

Embedded commands: When you mark out certain phrases that could stand as commands on their own by changing your voice tone or by gesturing so that others only unconsciously receive them.

Energy: The strength and vitality acquired for sustained physical or mental activity.

Eye-accessing cues: Movements with the eyes in certain directions that indicate visual, auditory, or kinesthetic thinking.
Visually Remembered: (eyes up to the right) seeing images of things seen before
Visually Constructed: (eyes up to the left) imagining images of things never seen before
Auditory Remembered: (eyes to the right side) remembering sounds heard before
Auditory Constructed: (eyes to the left side) hearing sounds never heard before
Auditory Digital: (eyes down to the right) talking to oneself
Kinesthetic: (eyes down to the left) Feeling emotions or tactile sensations

Frame: A context or way of perceiving something.

Future Pacing: The process of mentally acting out a future situation to ensure that a desired behavior will occur automatically and that a specific result will be acquired.

Generalization: The process by which parts of a person's internal experience get separated from the original experience and become a division of their own.

Identity: Our sense of who we are. It organizes our beliefs, capabilities, and behaviors into a single system.

Intention: The purpose or desired outcome of any behavior.

Internal Representation: The arrangement of information you create and keep in your mind in the form of pictures, sounds, feelings, smells, and tastes. To "recall" what your kindergarten classroom looked like, unless you're actually there, you will have to refer to your internal representation.

Kinesthetic: Relating to body sensations. In NLP, kinesthetic also refers to one's emotional and visceral sensations as well.

Leading: Changing your own behaviors with enough rapport for the other person to easily follow. It is a component of *pacing and leading* where you enter someone else's world and lead him or her to reach appropriate conclusions about his or herself and implement changes where needed.

Learning: The process of acquiring knowledge, skills, and experience.

Learning Strategies: Sequences of images, sounds, and feelings that lead to learning.

Learning Styles: Different preferred ways of learning.

Map (of reality): Each person's representation of the world built from their own perceptions or experiences.

Matching: Adopting parts of another person's behavior such as gestures, facial expressions, speech, or tone for the purpose of creating rapport with someone.

Meta Model: A model developed by John Grinder and Richard Bandler that identifies categories of language patterns that can be ambiguous. The Meta Model is based on common distortions, deletions and generalizations that people make. It implements clarifying questions that restore original meanings of messages.

Metaprogram: A determination of how we sort, orient to, or chunk our experiences.

Milton Model: The opposite of the Meta Model. The Milton Model uses vague language patterns to pace another's experience and access unconscious experience. It is based on the language used by famed hypnotherapist Milton H. Erickson.

Mirroring: Adopting other people's behaviors as if you were a mirror image. If you were facing someone who put his right hand on his forehead, you would put your left hand on your forehead to mirror him.

Mismatching: Adopting different patterns of behavior than another person for the purpose of breaking rapport.

Model: A description of how something works. A model can be a person whom we admire that has traits we wish to attain.

Modeling: The process of observing the successful behaviors of other people including their physiology, language, and skills so that they may be easily learned and duplicated by another.

Neuro-linguistic Programming (NLP): A set of techniques, axioms, and beliefs that are used as an approach to personal development. It was developed in 1973 by Richard Bandler and John Grinder and was based on the idea that mind, body, and language all interact to create an individual's perception of the world and that perceptions, and hence behaviors can be changed by the application of a variety of techniques.

Neurotransmitter: A chemical substance released at the end of a nerve fiber by the arrival of a nerve impulse, and by diffusing across a synapse, causes the transfer of the impulse to another nerve fiber.

Non-Verbal: Referring to the portion of our behavior that is communicated without words, such as tone of voice or gesturing.

Pacing: Gaining and maintaining rapport for a period of time while interacting with
another. You can pace ideas, beliefs, and behaviors. This is a component of *pacing and leading* where you enter another person's world and lead him or her to reach appropriate conclusions about his or herself and implement changes where needed.

Perceptual Filters: The unique ideas, experiences, beliefs and language that shape our model of the world.

pH: A figure in chemistry expressing the acidity or alkalinity of a solution on a scale in which 7 is neutral, lower values are more acid, and higher values are more alkaline.

Physiology: Relating to the physical parts of a person.

Preferred System: The representational system that a person uses most to think and to organize his or her experience.

Presupposition: A basic assumption needed in order for a representational system to make sense.

Rapport: The occurrence of people trading and/or sharing particular behaviors. It can happen naturally if two people spend enough time together or can be done consciously by matching and mirroring to enhance communication. Overall, it is an establishment of trust, harmony, and cooperation in a relationship.

Reframing: A process through which problematic behavior is separated from the positive intention of the internal program responsible for the behavior. New positive choices of behavior are then inserted by using the same internal program.

Representational Systems: How we code sensory information in our mind. They include the systems of: visual, auditory, olfaction (smell), and gustation (taste). They enable us to take in information, sort it, and use it.

Resources: Any means that can be brought to achieve an outcome. They can include but are not limited to thought, states, physiology, strategies, and experiences.

Secondary Gain: When a problematic behavior carries out a positive function on another level.

Sensory-based Description: Information that is directly observable and verifiable by the senses.

Softeners: A method of lessening the impact of a question but softening the tone of voice while asking.

State: The sum of all neurological processes within an individual at any particular moment in time. The state we are in affects our capabilities and interpretation of experiences.

Stimulus Response: An association between an experience and subsequent reaction. This is connected to Pavlov's experiment with the ringing of bells to stimulate the salivation in dogs.

Strategy: A set of specific behavioral and mental steps that are used to achieve a specific outcome.

Swish Pattern: A submodality process that programs your brain to go in a new direction. It is effective in transforming habits or destructive behaviors into healthy, constructive processes.

Submodalities: The minute classifications of external experience: a picture has brightness, depth, color and a sound has tone and pitch, etc.

Syntax: The sequence by which internal and external events are put together.

Tone: A modulation of the voice expressing a particular feeling or mood.

Trance: An altered state with an inward focus on a few stimuli. This is used to access unconscious resources and promote relaxation.

Values: The underlying components of what we find important and what drives our actions.

Visual: Relating to sight or the sense of sight.

Visualization: The process of seeing images in your mind.

BIBLIOGRAPHY

Bandler, Richard and John Grinder. *Frogs Into Princes*. Moab, Utah: Real People Press, 1979.

Bryant, Chris. 2001. Study Suggests First Handshakes and Good Impressions Really Do Go Hand-in-Hand. *University of Alabama* Vol. V: Issue I. http://research.ua.edu/archive2001/handshakes.html (accessed April 30, 2007)

Canfield, Jack, and Mark Victor Hansen. *Chicken Soup for the Soul: 101 Stories to Open the Heart and Rekindle the Spirit*. Deerfield Beach, Florida: Health Communications, Inc., 1993.

Cotes, John E., David J. Chinn, and Martin Raymond Miller. *Lung Function: Physiology, Measurement and Application in Medicine*. 6th ed. Maiden, Massachusetts: Blackwell Publishers, 2006.

Hall, Lynette J. *Healthful Eating.* Lincoln, Nebraska: iUniverse, 2006.

Hoeger, Werner W.K., and Sharon A. Hoeger. *Lifetime Physical Fitness and Wellness: A Personalized Program.* Belmont, California: Thomson Wadsworth, 2005.

Kamler, Kenneth. *Surviving the Extremes: A Doctor's Journey to the Limits of Human Endurance.* New York, New York: St. Martin's Press, 2004.

Kassing, Gayle, ed. *Introduction to Recreation and Leisure.* Champaigne, Illinois: Human Kinetics Inc, 2006.

McConnell, Charles R., *The Health Care Supervisor.* Gaithersburg, Maryland: Aspen Publishers Inc., 1993.

Meichenbaum, Donald, ed. *Human Adaptation to Extreme Stress: From the Holocaust to Vietnam.* New York, New York: Plenum Press, 1988.

Nay, Robert W. *Taking Charge of Anger.* New York, New York: The Guilford Press, 2004.

Seligman, Martin E. *Learned Optimism.* New York, New York: Knopf Publishing Group, 1991.

Time-Life Books Ltd. 1991. *The Mystifying Mind.* Virginia: Warner Books.

Weil, Andrew. Health and Healing. *New York, New York: Houghton-Mifflin Company, 1983.*

ABOUT THE AUTHOR

Sam Chauhan is a successful start-up entrepreneur, business innovator, honored sales strategist and experienced mortgage broker. Additionally, Sam has coached and motivated others in improving business tactics and increasing sales production and has an impressive clientele including employees from Mercedes-Benz, Countrywide, GMAC, Bank of America, Washington Mutual, Wells Fargo, as well as many other Fortune 500's. He is a frequent seminar speaker and a contributor for the nationally acclaimed *Mortgage Originator Magazine*. As a certified Master Practitioner in Neuro-Linguistic Programming, Sam specializes in teaching rapport and negotiation skills to business professionals and is a nationally published author of the highly circulated mortgage expert book *Loan Mastery*.

978-0-595-44876-0
0-595-44876-3

Printed in the United States
88107LV00004B/103-249/A